Hanging Out
for a Living

Mark Herdering

The Larry Czerwonka Company, LLC

Hilo, Hawai'i

First Edition — March 2014

Published by: The Larry Czerwonka Company
www.thelarryczerwonkacompany.com

Printed in the United States of America

ISBN: 0615970346
ISBN-13: 978-0615970349

Dedicated to Joe Spelleri
DECEMBER *4, 1924–*JULY *12, 1989*

Thanks for being the first person to encourage me to believe in myself and for being the best mentor anyone could hope to have. I miss you terribly, Pop.

Contents

PART THREE

PART FOUR

PART FIVE

Acknowledgements

Thanks to:

My friend Jordan Adler for showing me that one can hang out for a living. You are truly a master of the art.

Kody Bateman for creating the opportunity that has set me free to live and teach the hanging out for a living lifestyle.

Jolene Meadows for listening to my endless revisions night after night.

Mike Walsh and Kathie Nelson for indulging me in my early attempts at this book.

Brian Wright and Jim Hillas for your technical advice.

Steve Bergman and Ann Marcus for your feedback.

Vinnie Kisella at Indigo Editing for helping me knock the book into shape.

Dr. Ivan Misner for blazing the trail and the "Givers Gain" philosophy.

The Tea Zone, Broadway Cigar Co, Powell's City of Books, and the Oregon Culinary Institute for providing wonderful places to hang out in Portland.

The Portland Business Alliance for being such a great organization to network.

Mark Baker, Lisa Brumm, Frank Dane, Jerry Fletcher, Dale Henningsen, Suzy Oubre, Todd Kimball, Jason Snyder, Brian Taylor, Peter Wallmark, Eric Williams, Quincy Whitfield, Peggy Anderson, Tricia Guy, Joe Luman, Gabe Fasolino, Dan Pearson, Lori Bitter, Richard Fenton, Andrea Walsh, Michelle Sue, Larry Margolis, and the countless people too numerous to mention whom I've hung out with and whose conversations inspired and encouraged me.

PART ONE

ONE

A Really Bad Day

"You think you're better than me, man?" the unrelenting derelict begging me for spare change screams. "You don't know me. You don't know what I've been through. You rich guys think you're better than everyone else."

"Leave me alone!" I angrily reply.

On any other day I probably wouldn't even notice his obnoxious behavior. I'd be too busy holding my breath to avoid his booze-soaked stench. But this isn't any other day, and he's picked the wrong guy to harass. Today my world is falling apart, and I'm ready to unload on someone.

It's an unusually hot Pacific Northwest Monday afternoon. Infamous for its often cool, dreary weather, Northwest Oregon can occasionally experience short stretches of intense heat. This is one of those hot spells, and I'm having one of those days. I'm hot, angry, frustrated, and most of all, I'm scared. It's already the worst day of my life without this jerk frosting the cake

He could be in his mid-thirties, but it's hard to tell his age. His emaciated frame and sunken cheeks make him look like a living scarecrow. Bloodshot, light blue eyes and leathery skin suggest years of self-abuse. I turn to walk away, concerned his aggressive behavior may be fueled by a chemical agent more volatile than alcohol. Besides, I have to get to the next neighborhood on my sales route. But he's just warming up.

"Hey, I'm talkin' to you! You're not better than me. I'm a veteran, man!" he screams into my face with deliberate provocation. In a flash I find myself holding him by his grubby, checkered flannel shirt up against a dirty, white brick wall.

"Listen, scumbag, I'm having a really, *really* bad day," I seethe. "Get this through whatever's left of your brain. I don't care what you've been through. This morning I got served with a lawsuit, my boss is about to fire me from the crappiest job I've ever had, I'm so far behind on my bills I'll need two lifetimes just to catch up, and my wife is about to leave me. I was just trying to figure out the best way to kill myself when you interrupted my train of thought. I don't have any money, and if I did, I sure wouldn't give a damn cent of it to you!"

Insane with rage, I have him pinned hard against the wall, his feet dangling above the sidewalk. Struggling to speak, he submissively holds his arms out with palms open. "Sorry man. I . . . I don't want no trouble." His voice trembles through locks of greasy, dark hair draping down over his face. I let go as the adrenaline wears off and my faculties quickly return. He drops to the ground in a heap and cowers beneath me, waiting for what I might do next.

This isn't me. I have no idea who the monster is that just took over my body, manhandling the pathetic soul on the pavement below. Feeling dizzy I break down, collapse against the wall, and slump down to the sidewalk. With elbows resting on my knees and head buried in my hands, I begin to sob.

"Hey, man, how was I supposed to know? So what happened?" he asks with a sort of contrite curiosity.

Without lifting my head I cry into my hands, bemoaning the terrible sequence of events this morning that began with my wife, Karen, telling me she was leaving.

Finally tiring of the sound of my own sniveling, I just sit, paralyzed by the sudden release of my psychic pain. I'm content to stay here on the sidewalk in the middle of foot traffic, the inside of my eyelids a sanctuary from my troubles. The darkness accompanied by the white street noise of West Burnside bordering the south end of Portland's tiny China Town feels like safety, thousands of miles from this moment, this incident . . . this day.

After a few moments I become conscious of my body and the now awkward and uncomfortable position it's in. The sound of people passing me by on the sidewalk gets my attention. I raise my head to see the pedestrians glancing down with disgust at the two of us as they walk by. Looking over at him I see that his body position is nearly identical to mine. His arms wrapped around his knees, holding them close to his chest, he rocks back and forth while staring up at the sky with a vacant gaze. There's a very different personality operating here than the one that was screaming in my face just a moment ago.

"People don't think I'm smart, but I am," he babbles, still looking into the sky. "It's all a system, you know? Look what happened to you." I watch him as he rocks faster, pointing at me with a giggle that erupts into disconnected, tittering laughter. "Bustin' your ass and you're still in the same place as me. Yeah, man, I'M THE SMART ONE!" he screams into the street at no one.

He picks a cigarette butt up off the ground and puts it between his scabbed lips. Startled at his bizarre behavior, and horrified he might have a valid point, I quickly gather myself up, look down to see what I may have been sitting in, and brush off my pants. I can feel the wallet in my back pocket. Looking back, I see my momentary adversary turned sidewalk confidante still sitting and rocking far away in another reality. The realization that I'm only one minor disaster from joining him terrifies me. Under different circumstances he could be me and I could be him.

He's right; I don't know what he's been through. I pull out my wallet and examine the contents. Compared to him, I guess I am rich.

"Here. Sorry I went off on you," I say as I hand him my last four dollars. "It's not your fault I'm having a bad day." He snatches the money from my hand with a low growl and retreats back into a sort of catatonic daze. "You're welcome," I say sarcastically, continuing to swipe at the back of my trousers. He now seems to be completely unaware of my presence. Turning away, I begin the half-block walk up Burnside and around the corner to my car, distancing myself from the sound of his shouting at another passerby.

Exhausted, I step into my dilapidated Saturn parked in the late July sun. Hot air blasts from the dashboard vents as I start the ignition. I roll down the windows and wait for the air conditioning to kick in while I look over the sales contract of my first client, a web designer. I was on my way back from making my very first sale for Yellow Page USA when I'd been accosted. My new client reluctantly agreed to purchase the smallest ad available, a bold text quarter column for $45 per month, or $540 in annual revenue. I'm torn between the feeling of relief that I've finally made a sale and the realization that it won't make a dent in my quota. After spending two hours this morning making this one sale, I still have to draw up the ad and turn it in with the contract. Another hour of work yet for this one ad. God, I hate this job.

The air feels good as it begins to cool, working its way through my shirt. I take a moment to relax and close my eyes, embracing the dashboard breeze. As I do, the morning meeting with my manager begins to replay in my mind.

~Whatever You're Selling, We Don't Want It~

By nine o'clock it had already been the morning from hell. My heart raced and my mouth grew dry as I squirmed in the office chair while my manager, Jan, let out a sigh. She looked back and forth at some papers and then over her glasses at me.

"This just isn't going to work," she said. "In two months, you haven't turned in a single contract. What are you doing all day?"

"I'm doing my job, just like I was taught. Jan, as soon as I walk into a business in this monkey suit, carrying all that sales garbage, I'm told to get lost," I replied defensively, perhaps with a hint of anger. I was so frustrated at being confined to a sales process that had become an exercise in futility that I was past caring if I appeared insubordinate. I'm a husky, bald guy with a goatee and I shave what little hair still grows on my head. In a suit, I look something like a cross between a wrestler and a loan officer, so anyone who sees me come through their door correctly assumes that I'm there to sell something. There's little I can do to make my physical appearance any less threatening. I'm required to wear the suit and carry all the presentation materials. Heavy perspiration from the intense heat doesn't improve my image either.

She stared at me with an expression that looked like sympathy. She's lost many other recruits to the exact same problem. But the corporate policy is clear: if probationary employees can't make the grade, there are plenty of others out there looking for a job. As far as the company is concerned, it's just a game of numbers. The job goes to those who successfully play their game by their rules.

"Look, I can't fire you until your ninety days are up, but at this point I don't see how you're going to make the cut. It would save us both a lot of trouble if we just called it a day. You seem like a nice guy, and I'm sure there's something out there you're more suited for." I didn't respond. Unable to process the thought of again being out of work, I just stared out the window of the second story office and watched the Hawthorne Bridge as it rose over the Willamette River to allow a barge to pass.

After the meeting I left the building, took off my jacket and tie, unbuttoned the neck button of my shirt, and rolled up my shirtsleeves. What's the point in following the dress code if they're going to fire me anyway? I might as well be comfortable. Besides, there's no one supervising the field to make sure I'm sticking to the dress code. Logically, they'd sooner get rid of a guy that follows sales protocol and makes no sales than they would a guy that breaks the dress code but generates some revenue.

A passing police siren snaps me out of it. The air is as cool as it's going to get so I roll the windows back up, pull away from the curb, and head for the next neighborhood on my route, the Pearl District.

The Pearl is an interesting neighborhood just north of downtown. A few years ago it was a seedy, derelict area populated with abandon buildings and trash-strewn vacant lots. Gentrification has transformed the district into an eclectic mix of new glass and steel construction mixed with old industrial buildings converted to condominiums, theaters, restaurants and specialty shops. Today, it could easily be confused with the high rent retail district of any major city. Scottsdale, Arizona, comes to mind in this heat.

I arrive at a stretch of curb on NW Eleventh Avenue that's shaded from the bright sun by young trees and red brick condominiums. This looks like an ideal spot to take a break and eat my brown-bag lunch: a tuna sandwich, tangerine and bottled water. Though I haven't eaten all day, I'm not feeling very hungry. In fact, I'm not feeling well at all as I reach for the keys to shut off the ignition. The car shudders as the engine knocks before settling into silence. *That can't be good*, I think, fearing what might go wrong next.

Reaching into the brown bag that contains my now very warm lunch, I remove the sandwich and open the tepid bottle of water. Before I can take my first bite, a sickening pain erupts deep in my head and spreads to the back of my eyes. The telltale queasiness of yet another migraine headache creeps up as pinpricks of light start to pulsate at the periphery of my vision. It's only a matter of minutes before the indescribable pain and nausea of my all-too-familiar affliction hit full force. In an attempt to block out the light that severely aggravates my condition, I place a foldout cardboard sunscreen against the windshield, put on my sunglasses, and wet a tissue to wipe my forehead. Oh God, this is going to be a bad one.

~·The Tea Zone~

"You need to put some money in the meter, or I'm going to have to cite you."

"That's a strange thing for a dog to say," my dream mind remarks as I'm startled awake. Oblivious to the shorthaired woman on a bicycle wearing black shorts and a yellow shirt tapping at my car window, I take off my sunglasses and rub my eyes. As the fog slowly lifts from my brain, it slowly registers that there's a parking enforcement officer trying to get my attention. Still disoriented, I roll down the window.

"I said you need to put some money in the meter, or I'm going to have to cite you."

"Oh . . . right. Sorry, I wasn't feeling well. I guess I fell asleep."

"Are you okay, sir?"

"Yeah, I think so. I just had a doozy of a headache. But I feel all right now. Thanks."

In fact, my headache is gone, which is surprising because my migraines never give up that easily. I climb out of the car and walk to the parking meter several steps away, noticing that the shadows of the buildings have grown much longer now. *How long was I out?* I wonder. My stomach growls while I wait for the parking sticker to emerge from the meter. Famished, I return to the car, remove the bottle of water and my lunch bag. The car reeks of stale tuna and the bottle of water is warm to the touch. Concerned the sandwich may have gone bad, I toss it into a sidewalk trashcan and stuff the tangerine into my pocket.

A few steps up and across the street, I notice people sipping drinks at sidewalk tables covered by avocado green umbrellas. The words "Tea Zone and Camellia Lounge" are written in large white letters on a green banner that hangs like a flag outside a teahouse sandwiched between a furniture store and a bicycle shop. Hoping to find something to eat, I head for the door. An iced tea would sure hit the spot about now.

Stepping through the door, I'm engulfed by the smell of fragrant teas, fresh cooked pastries, and what must be the soup of the day. Haunting harp music fills the air. To my left, a middle-aged couple sits at a table, chatting over tea. At another, a young man dressed in black clothes, fluorescent green sneakers, and tattooed neck and arms, types away on a laptop. Ahead is the opening to a back room, which turns out to be the lounge.

"What can I get you?" a young woman in her early twenties with a big smile and mild southern accent asks from behind the counter. A blackboard menu describing an extensive selection of teas hangs on the wall. The words "Earl Grey/Almond" written in bright red chalk catch my eye.

"The Earl Grey Almond sounds tasty."

"Oh I love that!" she exclaims enthusiastically.

"How much for a medium?"

"That's $3.95."

Even though I gave away my last four dollars, my stomach wins a brief argument with my brain, rationalizing that I can use my credit card. I'm over my limit, but not all the charges have hit yet, I hope. *I'll figure it out later*, I tell myself. *I'm starving*.

"I'll take one of those, iced. And do you have anything to eat here?" I ask.

"We sure do!" she replies with a smile. She hands me a menu. "If you want, you can take a seat in the lounge, and I'll be right back to take your order."

"You know, I think you're the nicest person I've met all day. I love your energy!" I exclaim.

"Well, that's . . . like . . . the nicest thing anyone's said to me all day!"

"I'm Tyler. What's your name?"

"I'm Laura Lee. Pleased to meet you, Tyler."

As directed, I walk into the empty lounge, a dimly lit back room with small square tables and a built-in sofa bench wrapped around a back corner of the room. The music seems louder in here as I make my way around the tables to explore the dim space.

Distracted by the vibrantly colored abstract artwork that adorns the walls, I bump into a wooden bookcase that displays ornamental books and decorative knickknacks. Before I can react, a teapot hits the floor with a deafening crash. Startled, I watch helplessly as it bounces across the room in one direction, and its lid flies in another. The sound of footsteps and a panicked "Oh no! Oh no!" approach from the kitchen.

I chase down the lid while a gentleman runs in and picks up the teapot. "I'm so sorry!" I say, embarrassed.

With a sigh, he points to the dent on the side of the interesting piece of what, to me, appears to be just fancy bric-a-brac. "I can't sell this now!" he says with exasperation in what sounds like an Australian accent.

"I'm really sorry. I promise I'll pay for it," I hear my mouth say as my mind wonders how. "What is it?"

"It's a Moroccan teapot," he replies, shaking his head as if I had just destroyed an irreplaceable family heirloom.

In the dim light, I can't tell if the tarnished teapot is cheap pot metal or sterling silver. I know for sure it's something I neither need nor want. But his reaction leads me to believe I've just added another item to my long list of troubles. Numb to my mounting misfortunes, it occurs to me that, if nothing else, my luck today is at least consistent.

"That'll be $49.95, mate," he says matter-of-factly, placing the teapot on a table.

"Sure, no problem," I answer, taking a seat at the table. *Big problem*, I think. I'm relieved that the price wasn't considerably higher, but even at under fifty dollars, this is still another expense I really can't afford. Buying anything to eat now is out of the question.

He leaves the room, mumbling under his breath, as Laura Lee returns with a large glass of iced tea. "Oh, don't worry about Grant. We got a plumbing problem in the kitchen he's upset about. He's really a cool guy," she says, placing my tea on the table and then a hand on her hip. "Bummer about the teapot, though."

"So he's the manager?" I ask.

"He's the owner."

"Great," I mumble in frustration. I replace the lid, pick up the teapot, and stare at the dent.

"That's not so bad," she says. "It still looks beautiful."

Though not my taste, it does have a cheesy sort of charm.

"Is everything okay? You don't look too well."

"Yeah, everything's fine," I reply. "It's just been a very long day, and I wasn't prepared to buy this."

"Well, you just relax and enjoy your tea," she says with a sympathetic look. "You decide what you want to eat?"

"Looks like I'll just be having the tea, thanks."

"Well, if you need anything else, you just holler," she says with a lilt in her voice as she exits through the curtain door, leaving me alone in the dark lounge.

With a groan, I place the teapot back on the table and pull what is now a late afternoon snack out of my pocket: the warm tangerine. I'm so hungry that, as I peel the fruit, the sweet, pungent citrus smell hits me like steak smothered in garlic butter. I pop half in my mouth, pick up the teapot once again, and look it over more closely while I chew. Distracted by hunger, I hardly notice that it feels strange, heavier than it should be. It gives off a weird, tingling sensation, like electricity.

As I ponder my situation, concerns about my troubles erupt into a full-blown panic attack. Visions of impending financial disaster flash through my mind while I take inventory of my problems.

A Moroccan teapot, whatever that is. A cup of tea I have yet to pay for, and no money to buy anything to eat. Car's running rough. Karen's about to leave me. Behind on my bills. Being sued by the bank. Crippling migraines and no medical insurance. Thirty days left to generate $55,000 in sales or I lose my job.

"Fifty-five grand. Jeez! That's as much money as I've ever earned in a single year," I mutter aloud to myself. I begin to hyperventilate as the reality of my desperate situation crashes down upon me. I try to get a grip by thinking of something else. A simpler time, my senior year in high school, comes to mind, and I escape into my distant memory. "Man, money was never an issue back then. All I needed was enough dough to hang out with the gang at Speedy's taco stand," I mutter.

I'm a social creature. Even today I'd rather sit and have a conversation over coffee, or cigars when I can afford them, than do just about anything else.

Speedy . . . I wonder if that old guy is still alive, I continue to reminisce. *He made the best greasy food ever. That joint was such a cool place to hang out.*

I pick up a napkin from the table and unconsciously begin rubbing the damaged teapot, as if doing so will somehow fix the dent. Lost in thought, I fantasize aloud. "Wouldn't it be cool if I could make money by hanging out with people? Yeah, hanging out for a living. I wish I could hang out for a living."

With a jolt, the tingling feeling I barely noticed before intensifies. Startled, I quickly place the teapot back on the table. Something, steam or mist, pours out of the spout. The walls of the lounge seem to be pulling away from me, as if I'm getting smaller. The cloud of mist grows, boiling and changing colors from blues to purples to grays and back to blue. There's an odor, like frankincense. The mist fills the room and becomes so thick I can no longer see the teapot or even the table.

Two

At Your Service

Before I can react to my first instinct, which is to make a run for it, the mist dissolves with the same sound you hear after pouring a soft drink into a glass, like a million tiny carbonated bubbles fizzing away.

"At your service."

I blink to make sure I'm seeing clearly. Sitting across from me is a rotund man in his mid-sixties. He's wearing a short-sleeved, light blue, casual-style shirt unbuttoned to his navel, revealing a large chest and belly populated with dark, graying hair. On his wrist is a Timex watch just like the one my grandfather wore. Below a pair of khaki shorts he wears sandals on his otherwise bare feet. His olive complexion, classic Roman nose, and large dark eyes suggest Southern Europe or the Middle East. He has no visible neck, as if his lower chin were connected directly to his chest. A neatly trimmed black mustache and goatee frame a kind smile. There's a certain warmhearted, caring quality about his gruff, round face.

"I b-b-beg your pardon," I stutter.

"At your service."

Stunned, I look around the room to see who else might have witnessed the event. "Is this a joke?"

"Only if that is your wish."

I take a swig of tea and hold my eyes shut tight. As if things weren't bad enough, now I'm seeing things. I thought I'd hit bottom this morning when I broke down on the sidewalk, but this has got to qualify me for a padded room. *Okay, I'm coming completely unhinged, but panicking won't help*, I think, *so I might as well just go with it*.

I open my eyes to find he's still there, smiling at me with a kind and knowing expression, like a grandparent looking at a bewildered baby.

"You summoned me, did you not?" he asks with an unmistakably east coast accent.

"Look, I don't know what's going on. I didn't summon you. I was just sitting here minding my own business. Who are you? How did you get here?"

"You released me from my vessel," he replies while picking up the teapot and looking it over. "I'm obligated to grant one wish to whoever procures my freedom and states their wish with clarity."

I look into my tea closely and take a sniff, as if that will reveal some hallucinogenic I might have ingested.

"So you're a genie?"

"Not so loud!" he whispers as he looks around the room with his index finger to his lips. "There's no such thing as genies. I'm as human as you are. Besides, if I were a genie, you'd probably have found yourself in some circus act hanging feet-first over a hungry lion's mouth, begging for your life the instant you said 'I wish I could hang out for a living,'" he says, mocking me with a whiney, falsetto voice. "Look," he says softly, "let's just say I'm an expert at certain things, things you might need help with."

He sounds like he's from New York. His Buddha-esque physique, east coast accent, and gruff demeanor remind me of a film noir mafia character from the 1940s or 50s. In spite of his gruffness I instantly like him without knowing why. He has an irresistible, soft, and affectionate quality about him—like a caring uncle.

"Listen kid. . . ."

"Tyler."

"What's that?" he says, seeming annoyed at my interruption.

"My name is Tyler. Tyler Cirella. Call me Tyler."

"Oh yeah . . . right. Tyler." Though, when he says it, it comes out sounding like Ty-luh. "Look Tyler, you said you wished you could hang out for a living. You said you wanted to make money by hanging out," he says with a slightly frustrated tone.

I suddenly remember my daydream right before he appeared.

Leaning forward he points at me. "Youse weren't jerkin' me around were ya? I didn't come all this way to be jerked around."

"Come all what way? I don't even know who you are," I reply defensively.

He extends his thick hand. "Call me Oscar." Reluctantly, I shake it.

That same strange feeling I'd felt coming from the teapot surges through my hand, up my arm, and throughout my body. His thick hand feels like a baseball glove. The grip of his chubby, calloused fingers tells me these hands have done a lot of manual labor. I suddenly feel like everything's going to be okay, the kind of feeling a child might have being reunited with a parent after being lost in a strange and crowded place. As we shake, I can smell him, a sort of meaty aroma mixed with sandalwood and perhaps a trace of cardamom spice. Not in any way offensive but, to me, significant. How is it I can smell someone who can't possibly be here?

I look around the lounge again to see who else might be witness to what has taken place. The room is still empty. With a gulp I ask, "So, who are you, Oscar? How'd you get here?"

~Arkad and Bansir~

For the next few minutes, Oscar shares an incredible story. He describes having been a chariot builder in ancient Babylon nearly 2,500 years ago. As a young man he struggled, and, unable to pay his debts, found he and his family in indentured servitude with seemingly no way out. In a moment of despair, while preparing to make tea for his master, he pleaded aloud for guidance. It was then that a teacher by the name of Arkad mysteriously appeared before him. He explains that Arkad inhabited the teapot that had been given to him a hundred generations earlier, appearing before those who needed his guidance throughout the ages. Arkad had grown weary of the teapot and made a deal with Oscar, who at the time was referred to by his birth name, Bansir. In exchange for teaching him the secrets of success, Oscar would trade his mortality with Arkad, allowing Arkad to finish his days as a mortal man. Oscar would then carry on through the ages, teaching only those who were ready to learn and who agreed to follow his instructions exactly.

By the time Arkad's life ended, Oscar had amassed a massive fortune. As per their agreement, Oscar stopped aging at the moment of his mentor's death and carried on his work. Though preserved in his sixty-fifth year and weighing nearly three hundred pounds, the burly man was in perfect health, with the strength and agility of a man forty years younger, and he would remain so until he found his successor. He spent the next several years divesting himself of his fortune by helping the needy, funding the earliest schools of medicine, promoting business education, and investing in young entrepreneurs with no expectation of repayment while mentoring them along the way.

The large man pauses, his eyes glisten as he bites his lower lip. He continues the story by sharing the unforeseen curse of his arrangement with Arkad, the pain of outliving his wife, children, and longtime friends.

Finally, in what would be the ninety-ninth year of his life, Oscar had given everything away with the exception of the one material possession his teacher had given him: the teapot. The afternoon of the day Oscar gave away the last of his riches, he laid down for a brief nap. When he awoke, he was inside the teapot, with no sense of time or space, where he would remain until called forth decades later by the first person worthy of his guidance.

~So, You Want to Hang Out for a Living~

Stunned, I sit with my mouth open, unsure who is crazier, my hallucination or me. I swallow hard. "So now you're my teacher?"

"If you'll allow me," he replies with a tone of sincerity that moves me deeply.

Maybe I'm just particularly vulnerable today, but I'm overcome with fondness for the aberration that didn't exist a few minutes ago. I'll take a friend any way I can get one, even if he is just a figment of my imagination. I take a deep breath and clear my throat. "You know, Oscar, for someone from ancient Babylon, you sure sound a lot like my grandfather. He was from Brooklyn. Every once in a while, when he'd get excited, he'd say *youse* instead of *you*, just like you do."

"I'm automatically gifted with the ability to speak my student's language as soon as I emerge from my vessel," he says, staring at the teapot as he cups it with both hands. "I acquire a dialect of that language relatively close to the time and place where my assignment has brought me. Sometimes it carries over from one project to the next. My last two assignments were on the east coast of your country. I met my last student in Cleveland. I finally got him on his feet with a writing gig in Chicago." He cups his chin in thought, tapping his upper lip with his index finger. "Mandino was his name," he remembers.

It takes me a moment to process the familiar sounding name. "Og Mandino?"

"You've heard of him?"

"Heard of him? I've read every book he ever wrote . . . at least twice!"

"So the writing thing took off?"

"Oscar, Og Mandino went on to become an icon in the personal development field. He wrote over a dozen amazing books, all bestsellers. *The Greatest Salesman in the World* went on to become a word-of-of mouth phenomenon in the publishing industry."

"That's wonderful. He was a good kid to work with. I don't usually get to find out how my protégés turn out," he says, looking across the room with a far off gaze. "Poor guy was in a pretty bad way when I found him in some library. And not long before him there was another young fella I met in Brooklyn. As I recall he was actually from Colorado, but was in New York on business. Clayson was his name. Uhhh. . . . George!" he says snapping his fingers as he remembers.

"George Clayson was your student? The author of *The Richest Man in Babylon*?" I ask with astonishment, recollecting the names of the primary characters in the first chapter of the book I read only a couple of months ago: Arkad and Bansir. I raise my voice in surprise. "Oh my gosh! *The Richest Man In Babylon* was about you?"

"Where'd you think he got the idea for that?" Oscar says proudly, folding his arms with a smirk.

"So how did you get here? And what about—"

"Whoa!" he interrupts. "Look Tyler, you want my life's story, or do you want me to fulfill your wish?"

"But how do you fit inside that thing? How can you survive for eons?"

"The answer to all that would require a lengthy lesson in quantum physics. I got all the time there is, but you're 'bout halfway through all you're ever gonna get."

"Yeah, but . . . "

Leaning forward, his hands folded on the table, he looks me square in the eye. "Now you got one wish, kid. You want it to be an explanation of how I negotiate curved space-time or do you want to hang out for a living?"

"Can I have both?"

"One or the other."

I can't help thinking curved space-time sounds pretty cool. As if he can read my mind, Oscar looks directly at me, shaking his head back and forth, letting me know I'm perilously close to making a very bad choice.

"Hanging out?" I reply, still not entirely sure.

"Smart kid," he answers as he reaches over and pats me on the cheek. "So, you want to hang out for a living."

"Yeah!"

"Good, want to make sure I dressed appropriately."

I'm envious of Oscar's comfortable looking attire as I squirm in my sticky long-- sleeved shirt and slacks.

"We'll start with the basics, a journey of self-discovery. You know, who are you, what do you want, and how do you get it type stuff."

"I know I don't want to be a door-to-door salesperson."

"Sounds like a good place for us to begin. Though I suspect there's more going on with you than a dissatisfying job. Tell me what's troubling you, boy."

"Oh, Oscar, what's not troubling me would be an easier question to answer. My life's a mess."

"Talk to me," he says.

~It's Called Slarrefer Mutual~

"Oscar, today's been the worst day ever. I mean bad like a Woody Allen movie. If there's a news article in tomorrow's paper about a guy who was killed by a giant carp falling out of the sky, I'd be the guy."

Oscar raises one finger, signaling me to stop, gently grabs my left wrist and closes his eyes. "I don't see it happening," he says.

I force a smile. "Thanks." I can feel myself getting choked up. I take a sip of tea and clear my throat to compose myself.

"So what happened?"

I let out a sigh. "It's a long story."

"I got time."

"Okay." I say with a "you asked for it" tone.

"It all started back when I used to work as a welder. I had this kind of epiphany—a weird sort of daydream vision. I guess it was influenced by my Catholic upbringing. Anyway, I'm at the Pearly Gates after my death. Saint Peter goes over my chart before letting me in. When he's done, he looks at me with a raised eyebrow loaded with non-specific guilt and says, in this really deep, echoey sort of voice, 'So . . . looks like you sold off the most productive years of the life He gave you for twenty dollars an hour.'"

"Sounds like an enlightening moment."

"It was, Oscar! I knew right then I was destined for greater things, you know, but what? I've never had a clear calling; I've always been an employee. Working at a job is all I've ever known. The thought of giving up a regular paycheck was terrifying. But selling off the rest of my life one hour at a time scared me even more.

"Well, it was around that time I met my wife, Karen. Oscar, she's the most won-derful girl ever. I can still taste our first kiss," I recollect fondly. "Not long after we got married, the aerospace industry collapsed, and I was laid off from my welding job near Seattle. At the time, she really encouraged my dreams. We moved to Portland after she landed an administrative job with a small company down here. She doesn't get bene-fits, but the pay's okay. Besides, rent's a lot lower here than it is in Seattle.

"So, with Karen's support, I tried various entrepreneurial pursuits. You know, network marketing, no-money-down real estate investing, day trading, you name it. I financed it all with credit cards, but I never made a cent.

"Then, a couple of years ago, I started getting these really bad headaches. My doc-tor told me the symptoms sounded like migraines. I asked him how we could tell. He gave me some pills and said if they worked, it was a migraine."

"Sounds logical."

"I suppose. Well, the pills work. I mean they knock out the headaches. But there's still this residual exhaustion that lasts for about a day, like I was in a chess marathon or something. Anyway, I'm getting the headaches three or four times a week now. It's crippling. I don't have insurance, and the pills cost twenty-five bucks each. I asked the doctor if there was anything else we could do. He said I should get an MRI and some other tests in case it was something serious, but I'm so deep in debt the additional ex-pense is just out of the question. So I was forced to find a 'real job,' as Karen puts it, to get medical insurance."

I swallow another sip of tea and become momentarily distracted by the glow of the curtains on the wall behind Oscar. The eerie, piano-driven bass riff and distant saxo-phone of Traffic's "Low Spark of High Heeled Boys" bleeds from the dark lounge's speaker system, providing the soundtrack to a moment I can't imagine becoming any more surreal. The brief impulse of slapping myself to see if this is all a dream passes quickly, and I continue my story.

"About the same time I took this job, I was introduced to another business opportunity. Oscar, this is the one. It's like everything I've failed at was just to prepare me for this."

"Tell me about it."

"It's called Slarrefer Mutual. They provide life and long-term care insurance and financial products and education to their clients through a network marketing business model. One of the smart things I did a while back was to get state certified to sell life insurance, so when a friend took me to their business presentation, it seemed like a perfect fit. I really like this company. They're teaching me about finance and investing and helping me pass the Series 6 Exam so I can sell variable annuities. Most of all, I love the people and the culture of the company. There's something different about this one. I'm excited about it, and I really want to share it with others. It's what I'm supposed to be doing."

I rest my elbow on the table and lower my forehead into my palm. "But that's where I really screwed up. Oscar, Karen and I had our worst fight ever this morning."

"What do you mean?"

"I spent $759 for my distributorship and didn't tell her. She saw it on the credit card statement this morning and went through the roof. I'm afraid she's going to leave me. I can't blame her for being angry. She was doing fine until she met me. I'm thirty-five years old, drowning in debt, no insurance, no savings, and no career. It's like the last few years have been just a bunch of bad choices and wrong turns that led me to today."

I fall back in my chair, let my arms dangle at my sides, lean my head back with a sigh, and stare at the ceiling as I finish the story.

"The fight with Karen was just the beginning. After our blowup, I get into the car for work, and before I can close the door, this guy comes up and asks me if I'm Tyler Cirella. Before I even finished saying yes, he hands me an envelope and says, 'You've been served.' It's a lawsuit by the bank for falling behind on a loan. I was so distracted as I read it that I spilled my coffee in my lap. That made me late for work. I was supposed to be in the office at eight thirty for a sixty-day review with my boss. On the way there, I got pulled over for speeding on I-5 through the Terwilliger curves. A $280 ticket!"

"This does sound like a Woody Allen movie."

"Oh, it gets better. Now I'm really late when I show up with a big, wet, dark stain in my crotch. My boss let me have it. She asked me to quit so she didn't have to fire me. If I don't hit my quota in the next thirty days, I'm out of a job."

I sit silently for a moment before continuing, hesitant to tell him what happened next.

"Is that it?"

"No."

He rolls his eyes. I can't tell if it's empathy for how bad my day has been, or if he's wondering how much more of this he's going to have to listen to.

"Oscar, I did something terrible this morning. I attacked a homeless guy."

"Why would you do such a thing?"

"I was walking down Burnside with all this stuff going around in my head when he comes out of nowhere, really obnoxious like, begging me for money. I tried to ignore him, but he just got really belligerent. I couldn't take it. I flipped out and threw him against a wall. I don't know what happened next. It's like I blacked out. Next thing I know I'm on the sidewalk sitting next to him pouring my guts out about how screwed up my life is."

"So what happened?"

"I finally realized I was sitting on the ground with a crazy homeless guy. I got up, pulled myself together, then gave him the change I had and left."

"And why did you do that?"

"I don't know. To make up for what I did to him. Or because I felt bad for him. Or because I'm not that far from being in his shoes. Just seemed like the right thing to do, I guess. You know, karma."

"Hmmm . . . interesting," Oscar replies, removing a small notepad and a stubby pencil from his shirt pocket.

"I hate this job, Oscar." I start to sob. "But I can't afford to lose it. I really need the medical insurance. We're in so deep I can't even tread water anymore. Now it looks like Karen's going to leave me for good. I wish I was dead."

"If today is, in fact, the worst day of your life, then you, my friend, lead a charmed life indeed," he says, touching the tip of the pencil to his tongue and jotting something down. "I wonder if an afternoon slaving in the Hanging Gardens under the whip of Nebuchadnezzar's guards might make you a bit more appreciative of your circumstances," he says, stroking his chin, as if he can make that happen, and is seriously considering it.

"I don't think that'll be necessary. I get your point."

THREE

A Crisis Is a Terrible Thing To Waste

"All right, kid, I think I get the picture. You've gotten yourself into a pretty tight spot, and only you can get yourself out. As long as you understand that, then I believe I can offer you some guidance."

"I'll take any help you give me."

"Very well, let's get to work. Lesson one: get into the habit of being the very best you can at whatever you do, even if it's not what you want to do."

"Oscar, I've got less than a month to be better than my best or I'm out of a job."

"That's wonderful!" he exclaims. "Nothing like a good crisis to find out what your best really is. A crisis is a terrible thing to waste."

"Huh . . . ?" I grunt with self-righteous contempt, certain he doesn't appreciate the gravity of my situation.

"My boy, the universe has a wonderful way of providing for us the answers we need through uninvited challenges. I submit to you that you created this situation in order to attract your greatest opportunity for success. Most mortals miss the gift of a personal crisis. Yet there has never been one created that did not hold the way to an abundant future. Allow me to give you a contemporary example you may more easily understand."

"Okay." I pick up my tea and settle into my seat.

~Fear Factor~

"On the device you call a television there was once a program, a reality show. I believe it was called *Fear Factor.*"

"Yeah, I remember that."

"Explain it to me," Oscar says as he leans back, folds his arms, and closes his eyes.

"Well . . ." I begin by looking up to the ceiling trying to remember the show's premise. "Participants in the show were subjected to frightening situations that confront basic human fears like heights and insects. Contestants would compete against each other by completing a scenario in the least amount of time or by enduring a situation for a specified amount of time. Whoever took the longest, or quit, was out. The person who survived all the fear challenges was the winner. I think they won money."

"Very good," Oscar says opening his eyes. "Now explain to me what strategy you think someone would have to employ to win such a competition."

"I guess the game itself had to be rigged. If there were any real danger, I don't think they'd be able to do it, 'cause of liability reasons if nothing else," I muse. "So I s'pose it's a mental thing. For example, eating cockroaches or a cow's eyes . . . intellectually we know that those aren't poisonous or harmful, but they are disgusting, at least to most westerners. So it seems like the strategy to win would be to somehow embrace the experience, you know, to eliminate any hesitation. Otherwise you'd instinctively be repelled and then hesitate, causing you to slow down and, therefore, lose."

I look at him to see if my explanation is satisfactory.

"Excellent." Oscar nods his head in the affirmative. "I particularly like your use of the word *embrace*. You must embrace your circumstances for they are much like the wrapping that conceals a wonderful gift; a gift much greater than a meager cash prize."

"Yeah, but I could use the cash." I turn out my pockets in a lighthearted gesture.

"Riches beyond your wildest dreams await you, monetary and otherwise, if you're prepared to embrace your situation for the gift it truly is."

I feel inspired by Oscar's reframe of my situation. If, in fact, this predicament is actually the answer to my quest for an easier and more abundant life, I'm ready to meet it head on.

~ What Does Hanging Out for a Living Mean? ~

"Let's get back to your wish which summoned me here. What, exactly, does hanging out for living mean?"

"I guess it means a lifestyle that allows me to be with the kind of people I want to be with, doing the things I want to do, and yet somehow generate a decent income from it—as opposed to having to take time away from what makes me happy in order to make money," I reply uncertainly.

Oscar strokes his chin while pondering my answer. "I'll accept that definition provided that you understand your wish must be in accordance with a universal law as fundamental as gravity," he says with a serious tone as he leans toward me, looks directly into my eyes, and pokes me in the chest. "You must live this lifestyle in service to others."

I smile. Not only do I understand, but it's also the missing piece that now brings clarity to my otherwise vague picture of what hanging out for a living means. "Yeah!

That's it Oscar. I want to hang out, but I want to make a difference. I want to hang out . . . in service to others. I love that!"

"Wonderful!" he replies in an animated gesture, throwing his arms open as he leans back. "Let's start by giving hanging out for a living a definition you and I can both agree upon. Hanging out for a living isn't an occupation or a business, but is instead a philosophy and a method of conducting business for the highest and best good of all. A method that makes generating business *seem* like hanging out."

"That works for me."

"Good. Can we also agree that *hanging out* and *hanging out for a living* are not the same thing?"

"Yeah, that makes sense. Hanging out with a friend or relative for no reason other than having a beer and enjoying the sunset doesn't sound like much of a vocation. So I guess I have to figure out how to serve people by hanging out with them."

"Correct. Hanging out for a living must be about relationships—specifically, business relationships. Business relationships that are based on something other than business."

"If they're not based on business, what are they based on?"

"The pleasure of the other person's company. In order to successfully hang out for a living, one must focus on the relationship rather than the monetary transaction."

~The Art of Relational Reciprocity~

"Oscar, I'm open to all you have to teach me. But I'm getting a little nervous now. The pleasure of another person's company isn't going to pay my rent," I protest.

"Think about it, boy. Right now millions and millions of dollars are being made on golf courses all over your country by people who aren't working as much as they're . . ." He gestures to me to finish the sentence.

"Hanging out?"

"Precisely! However, building a business by hanging out will require taking the metaphoric golf game to a different level, but I assure you it can be done," he says smugly while buffing his fingernails on his shirt. "It's going to require that you master the art of relational reciprocity."

"What does that mean?"

"To use a simpler term, giving and receiving referrals. Though what I'm going to share with you goes deeper than that."

"I didn't realize that was an art, Oscar. I thought that a client either refers others to me or they don't."

"The kind of referral I'm talking about isn't a random recommendation by a satisfied client."

"I guess I have a lot to learn, 'cause that's the only kind of referral I know of."

"Not to worry. Mastering this art isn't difficult. In terms of importance, it's ninety percent philosophy and ten percent mechanics. We've already defined the philosophy, which is that you can only hang out for a living if you do so in service to others. Any deviation from that philosophy will lead to certain failure in your endeavors. Do I make myself clear?"

"Yes," I reply nervously. Oscar has some kind of parental authority over me. When he speaks directly to me like that I get a feeling like I'm nine years old, and I'll end up over his knee if I don't obey.

"That philosophy is easier to recite than it's going to be to practice. But you have a wonderful, giving nature kid. I wouldn't be here if I didn't think you were up to it. It's the other ten percent, the mechanics, which I'll teach you. I'm going to share with you an entirely new way of looking at how you market yourself and your business. However, you're going to have to suspend your beliefs while I take you through a short series of lessons, each one building upon the others. The challenge for you will be that it won't all come together until the final lesson. In the meantime, you're going to have to trust me and do what I tell you."

~Advanced Souls~

"I want to trust you Oscar . . . "

"But . . . ?" he asks, anticipating the rest of my sentence.

I lean on the table and stare directly into his deep black eyes. "But how can I trust you when you tell me you're as human as I am? Oscar, humans don't live in teapots, especially humans your size—no offense. And humans don't materialize out of thin air, or live for 2,500 years, or negotiate curved space-time . . . whatever that is."

"The advanced ones do," he says with a defensive tone. "Any advanced soul with faith and patience can do it."

"And how does someone become an advanced soul?" I ask indignantly.

"There's a serious flaw in your question. It presupposes one isn't already an advanced soul."

"I'm not following you."

"The appropriate question would be 'How does one remain an advanced soul?' We are all born into this life as advanced souls. The challenge of life is to live into the mission that we chose for ourselves before our birth. Most, however, forget their self-appointed mission once they become immersed in the material, sensory world."

"So I could be an advanced soul and do the things you do?"

"Everyone can."

"How?"

"Okay, I'll give you this much, but then we have to get to work. One must live a life of service and contribution. It must be a life that fulfills the self, yet leaves the world a better place.

"Imagine that you were born with a self-designed life. You chose virtually everything about your life prior to your birth . . . your parents, siblings, country, triumphs, defeats, sufferings, and bliss. You chose your most unpleasant moments, your disabilities, and your gifts. You designed your life, start to finish, in order to advance your soul to the next level. By attaining the next level you're invited to return to the Earthly realm, if you so choose, in order to serve further.

"Anyone can live as a bodhisattva or by the example of the Khristós. Most, however, don't because they forget their enlightened nature. They forget that they chose their circumstances and instead devolve into victims of their circumstances."

Oscar has just given me the single most empowering way of thinking I've ever heard. "Wow . . . ! I think you just rocked my world Oscar. So what about the curved space-time stuff you were telling me about. How do you learn that?"

"They give you a book."

"A book? What kind of book?"

"The Negotiating Curved Space-Time for the Advanced Soul Handbook of course."

"You're pulling my leg, right?"

Oscar just shrugs his shoulders and gives me an expressionless stare.

"Oh, Oscar, don't do this to me. Is anything you just told me true?"

"It doesn't matter."

I can't help raising my voice in frustration. "What do you mean it doesn't matter?"

"I mean it doesn't matter. Just living into the belief that you designed your life in advance of your birth forces you to find a lesson and opportunity for growth in every obstacle, challenge, and disaster that life presents you with. You also get to experience exponentially multiplied satisfaction in the high points of your life, since you must take credit for those as well. Doesn't matter if it's true. Just live as if it is. Try it. If you don't find purpose, growth, and accelerated momentum in every aspect of your life, you can always go back to being a victim."

I can't deny how empowering this philosophy of personal responsibility could be, though I imagine living into it is easier said than done. "Oscar, this is the strangest conversation I've ever had in my life. But at this point I've got nothing to lose. I'm open to anything. I'll do whatever you say."

"Very good! Tomorrow we'll cover the next lesson: being the solution to a problem," he says, hammering the tip of his index finger into the coffee table.

Perplexed, I furrow my brow. "Being the solution to a problem?"

"Meet me here tomorrow morning—say nine?—and we'll talk about it."

"I'll be here!"

"That's my boy," he says, reaching over and gently shaking my shoulder. "Tonight you get yourself some sleep."

"I'll try." I take one last gulp of tea, get up from the table and pick up the teapot. It feels much lighter than before. "Guess I'd better go pay for this," I say with a sigh as I tuck it under my arm.

"Might be the best investment you ever made."

I walk to the front where Laura Lee cheerfully finishes ringing up another customer and takes my check.

"That'll be $54.95."

I hand over my credit card, praying the transaction won't hit until I can put some money in my account.

"Was everything okay?"

"Yeah, the tea was great. But the conversation was amazing!"

"The conversation?" she asks quizzically.

"Yeah. With the gentleman sitting at my table in the lounge."

She raises her eyebrows and shrugs. "Okay. Well, you have a great night!"

"You too. Thanks Laura Lee."

I walk back into the lounge to say goodbye to Oscar, but he's nowhere to be seen. I realize the teapot feels much heavier again, along with the tingling feeling. Inquisitively I place it back on the table and remove the lid to look inside. I see nothing but darkness broken by a faint reflection of light off the bottom.

FOUR

Being the Solution to a Problem

"Can I get you something?" asks a female voice from behind the counter.

"Umm . . . sure. I'll have a Power Plant," I answer, referring to a strong herbal lemon brew described on the blackboard.

"Hot or cold?"

"Hot please. And could you please bring two cups. I'm expecting someone."

"You got it. By the way, I'm Janie."

"Nice to meet you, Janie. I'm Tyler."

"Aren't you the gentleman who bought the teapot yesterday?"

"Oh . . . yeah. You know about that?"

"I was in the kitchen when we heard it hit the floor," she explains. "That was my husband, Grant, you spoke to. Hope he wasn't too hard on you. We were having a tough day yesterday. He was upset about a plumbing problem we were dealing with."

"Yeah. That's what Laura Lee told me."

She looks over her shoulder toward the kitchen, then back at me. "That old teapot's been up on the bookshelf for years," she whispers. "No one was going buy that thing anyway. He shouldn't have stuck you with it. If you want, I'll take it back and refund your money."

"Thanks, Janie, that's really kind of you. But I offered to pay for it. Besides, I've actually become kind of attached to it."

"Really?" she says with a surprised expression. "Okay. Well, if you'd like to take a seat in the lounge, I'll be back there in a minute with your tea."

It's a little before nine o'clock on Tuesday morning as I take a seat in the dark lounge of the Tea Zone. Soft jazz oozes from the sound system while the eerie light emanating through the decorative curtains that cover the corner behind me dissolves from light green into deep blue. Again, I'm the only customer here.

While I wait for my tea, I can't keep from entertaining my doubts and begin to wonder if Oscar will show up. *Why am I here?* I ask myself. *I've only got twenty-nine days to go. I should be out drumming up business.*

It occurs to me that I didn't bring the teapot, remembering it's on the floor of the front passenger side of my car where I left it last night. *Is Oscar still in there? He didn't say I needed to bring it. Perhaps it was just obvious, so he didn't say anything.*

My train of thought is interrupted by the arrival of my tea. "Careful, it's hot," says Janie as she sets the pot on a ceramic trivet. "Let me know if you need anything else."

"Thanks," I respond.

As she leaves, my mind begins to race. *I must be crazy. What am I doing here? It must've all been some kind of dream. You actually think some 2,500-year-old guy built like a human bulldog came out of that teapot and had a conversation with you?* I panic about both the time I'm wasting here and the prospect of losing my sanity. *You idiot. You could've gotten your money back.*

Giving into my trepidation, I ignore my tea and reach down to pick up my briefcase in a rush to leave. Only a brief second passes before I raise my head above the table and discover Oscar sitting across from me, eating a croissant.

"You don't give a guy much of a chance, do you?" he says through a full mouth as he chews.

"Oscar! How did you? I mean when did you?" Unable to find words, I stammer, feeling both stunned and relieved at his sudden appearance.

He licks his fingers, far more concerned about his food than about giving me a satisfactory explanation. "Didn't think I'd show, eh?"

"I started thinking yesterday afternoon didn't even happen."

"Not to worry," he says, dismissively waving his hand. "Sit yourself back down. Unwind a little." His demeanor is so relaxed it makes me think of a Sunday afternoon in a hammock. "You get some rest last night?"

"Sort of. Karen let me have it with both barrels. She made it pretty clear that I'm on probation. Any more stupid financial moves, and I'll be the one moving out. To make her point she told me that she and the bedroom are off limits until further notice. So I spent the night on the couch. I woke up with a horrible stiff neck this morning."

"That's rough, kid," Oscar responds sympathetically. "My wife and I had a few rows in our early days. Of course, in those days women didn't have the option of moving out. They had no choice but to live with the consequences of a husband's bad choices. My poor bride ended up an indentured servant, cleaning out the bathing facilities of our masters, due to my early entrepreneurial missteps."

"Wow! Now *that's* rough."

"Indeed. No amount of slave labor I was forced to endure came close to the shame I felt for the suffering and degradation my follies put that most wonderful of women through."

"At least she ended up being the wife of the richest man in Babylon," I reply facetiously.

"No amount of success is worth such a price," Oscar answers with a pained expression.

"Sorry. I didn't mean to—"

"It's okay, kid," Oscar interrupts. "But take it from someone who knows, putting your wife's happiness and comfort at risk is not an acceptable price to pay for success."

He quickly changes the subject. "Okay, enough lamenting the past. What do you say we get started with our lesson? You ready to begin?"

"Am I ever!" I exclaim as I settle into my seat.

Oscar closes his eyes and sits perfectly still, leaving me in an awkward silence. Several moments pass before he gradually opens them. "Today you're going to become a problem-solver as opposed to a 'doer' of your job."

"Huh?"

"We're going to explore the problem that you solve, as opposed to what you do. You see, no one cares what you do."

He's found a tender spot on my ego. "What do you mean no one cares what I do?"

~I Make Broken Cars Go~

"Allow me to demonstrate. Imagine you're in line at the hors d'oeuvres table at a business event like a chamber of commerce mixer."

"Okay."

"You notice the guy standing next to you is wearing a name tag that says *Bob*, and underneath is written *Bob's Automotive*. You extend your hand and say . . . " Oscar gestures toward me for a response.

"Hi, I'm Tyler?" I'm playing along but have no idea where this is going.

"Right. And he says to you . . . ?"

"Uhhh . . . I'm Bob. Pleased to meet you?"

"Good. And you reply?"

I'm beginning to get the role-playing exercise. "What do you do, Bob?"

"And Bob replies . . ."

"I'm a mechanic."

"And you reply?"

"Umm. . . ." I stammer trying to think of what to say.

"Exactly!" Oscar says throwing up his arms. "Kind of awkward, isn't it?"

"Yeah . . . well . . . I mean . . . I'm sure I'd say something if it was a real conversation. A mechanic would be a good Yellow Page customer."

"At which point Bob the mechanic would probably pick up on your desire to turn the conversation into a sales pitch. Bob's not interested in your directory," Oscar says rather bluntly.

"That's because he's not aware of how I can help him," I reply confidently, falling back on the canned response I learned in my sales training.

"And Bob's thinking the exact same thing. He knows you have a car. If you have a car, you need him."

"But I already have a mechanic."

"You're simply not aware of how he can help you," Oscar counters, using my own sales logic against me. "Now you're both on the defensive, and you'd say whatever you had to say to get out of the conversation and move on to someone else."

"Yeah . . . I guess that's true."

"How often do you experience this kind of conversation when you're at a networking event, like a chamber mixer?"

"Every time I've been to one," I say sheepishly.

"And how do you feel about such conversations at these events?"

"It feels uncomfortable. But it's a game of numbers, Oscar. I'm just meeting people until I find someone who wants what I have to offer. That's what everyone does. That's what happens at networking events."

"And you're going to change all that," Oscar says, poking me in the chest to emphasize the point, a gesture that's becoming familiar. If another guy did it, I'd be tempted to break his finger. But when Oscar does it, there's something endearing about it.

"When someone asks 'What do you do?' what is your response?"

"I sell yellow-pages advertising."

"That answer will suffice on a tax return or loan application. However, in a situation like a networking event, you're never to use that response again."

"What do you mean, Oscar? You asked me what I did, and I told you."

"And I'm telling you no one cares what you do. In fact, telling someone what you do is like turning off the switch to their attention span. Allow me to demonstrate. Let's go back to our conversation with Bob."

"Okay."

"Pretend I'm Bob. Ask me what I do."

"Nice to meet you Bob. So . . . what do you do?"

"I make broken cars go."

I raise my eyebrows, not expecting that answer. "So how do you do that?"

Instead of answering the question, Oscar just smiles. "Why did you ask that?"

"Because I was interested, I guess."

"Weren't you interested during the first conversation when Bob's reply was that he's a mechanic?"

"Now that I think about it, I wasn't."

"What was the difference?"

I stroke my chin. "Well, when Bob said he was a mechanic, I assumed I knew it all. It's like if I see a sign that says *mechanic,* I know what goes on there. But when I heard 'I make broken cars go,' I remembered times when my car wouldn't go and just associated him with getting the car moving, I guess." I give Oscar a puzzled look to let him know I'm not sure of my answer.

"Perhaps I can articulate it better. *Mechanic* is just a word, especially to a mind that is busy trying to find customers, meet the right people to talk to, and get some of the avocado and shrimp hors d'oeuvres before they're all gone. However, a broken car is an experience everyone in your mechanical age can relate to. And the thought of 'a broken car going,'" Oscar says making quotations signs with his fingers, "is something everyone who has ever experienced a broken car can appreciate."

"Yeah, now I actually have an interest in Bob, even if my car is working just fine ... and I want to continue the conversation."

"Now you're getting it. Which Bob would be more memorable to you, Mechanic Bob or I Make Broken Cars Go Bob?"

"Broken Cars Bob, of course."

"Good. So let's sum this up with an exercise. When you're attending a networking event, the answer to the question 'What do you do?' is best answered with a simple, one sentence description that speaks to the solution to a problem. Resist the temptation to sound sophisticated and intellectual. It's your ego that finds satisfaction in being an expert. However, it's your wallet that will be satisfied by keeping your message simple. Let me ask you a question that should help you discover what to say when someone asks you what you do. What might you overhear at a party that would prompt me to suggest that the person doing the complaining should contact you for a solution?'"

"In my case, if someone, say a plumber, complained that the business line stopped ringing like it used to."

"Okay. So how do you solve that problem?"

"I make prospects call you?"

"Very good! However, the word *you* sounds a bit direct to me. What do you think?"

"Hmmm . . . I think I see what you mean. How about 'I cause businesses to get calls from prospects'?"

"Congratulations, you've just discovered what you should tell people when they ask what you do. You might even tighten it up by saying 'I cause businesses to get calls from qualified prospects.'"

"Oooh, that's good!" I quickly write Oscar's response down.

"Can you give me another?" he asks.

"I make business lines ring?"

"Not bad. One more."

"I make businesses easy to find?"

"You've got it!" he says while reaching over to shake my hand. "Now I'm going to qualify this portion of our lesson. I said no one cares what you do to make a point. If, however, you were being introduced to someone who did have a specific interest in you and your business, or was in the same or a related field, you would, of course, simply tell them what you do."

"I think I get the distinction, Oscar. It only makes sense to answer the question 'What do you do?' with the solution to a problem in the context of an event where people know little or nothing about me or my profession."

"Well said. It just comes down to being aware of where you are and whom you're talking to. Now let's look at the bigger picture of why knowing the problem you solve is so important. Being the answer to a problem, rather than being the doer of a job, is going to be critical to your long-term survival."

"How so?"

"Allow me to explain with a story."

~A Cure for Darkness~

"Late in your nineteenth century, there was a candlemaker who served a large population in the New England area of your country. He employed many people, had an impressive distribution network, a superior manufacturing process, and had the financial means to purchase raw material in bulk for far less than his competition. Therefore, he dominated the candle market. However, since he focused all his energy on what he did, rather than on the problem he solved, he soon lost his business to a better solution to the problem."

Oscar lets out a sigh, closes his eyes, and folds his hands on the table. I can't stand the awkward pause and blurt out, "So what happened? Why did he go out of business?"

He slowly opens his eyes as he responds, his words coming out at half the speed they did a moment ago. "I told you, the candlemaker focused on what he did rather than solving a problem. When one promotes what they do rather than being the solution to a problem, sooner or later they must either drastically transform their business model or cease doing business all together. I've given you all the information necessary to understand the demise of the candlemaker."

"I'm missing it. If people needed candles, and he was the top guy in the industry, why would he lose all his customers?"

Oscar sits motionless with his hands still folded on the table and an expression that says "Figure it out for yourself" as clearly as if he were speaking the words.

I roll my eyes and let out a sigh. "Okay . . . he lost sight of the problem he solved." I recap aloud, stroking my chin as I look up in thought. "People needed candles; that was the problem. And he fulfilled that need better than anyone. So why would he lose his customers?" I stare back at Oscar with a look that begs for another clue.

"My boy, your fate is assured to be that of the candlemaker if I don't allow you to figure this out on your own." He closes his eyes again, as if he'll just take a nap until I get it.

I squirm in my seat, realizing I could be here all day at this rate. "Okay, I guess I need to figure out why people would stop buying candles from him," I think aloud. "The problem he solved was candles—wait—NO! The problem he solved had nothing to do with candles. Candles are what the candlemaker did!" I exclaim and snap my fingers in an "ah-ha" moment. Oscar remains motionless with his eyes closed, but I can see a slight smirk begin to appear on his face. "Okay . . . I'm getting it. Candles are what the candlemaker did, not the problem he solved. People needed candles to light their homes. That's it! The problem was dark homes, not the need for candles. But candles did solve that problem."

"Until . . . ?" Oscar says, softly coaxing me.

"Until the lightbulb came along?"

"Bingo," Oscar responds, opening his eyes. "Continue."

"The problem the candlemaker solved was to bring light to dark places."

"Very good!"

"So manufacturing candles was simply how he solved that problem," I say to myself as I ponder the candlemaker's dilemma. "As soon as electricity and the lightbulb came along, his business was obsolete. But Oscar, even if he had been focused on lighting dark places instead of manufacturing candles, that wouldn't have prevented the lightbulb from wiping out the candle business."

"You're correct. However, the opportunity to exploit the advent of the electric light by investing his resources into becoming a manufacturer and distributor of lightbulbs was available to him. He had the financial resources and the customer base. But the candlemaker saw the better solution to the problem as a threat rather than an opportunity. That's what happens when one focuses on what they do rather than the problem they solve. Had he been focused on bringing light to dark places, rather than making candles, he would have seen his business evolve with the lightbulb rather than die at the hands of progress."

"I get it. Wow, Oscar, you're right; it has nothing to do with what you do. It's all about the problem you solve. If people can see that you have the solution to their problem, *then* they will take an interest in doing business with you. But they will always move to the best solution to their problem, regardless of how good we are at what we do."

"Exactly. Allow me to give you a more contemporary example of this," he says before pausing to take a sip of tea. "For over one hundred years your industrial landscape has been dominated by oil companies. Due to the fact that oil is a limited resource and its consumption creates environmental havoc, that industry finds itself in a position not dissimilar from that of our friend the candlemaker. However, to their credit, some of those companies have begun to realize that they are in the business of solving a problem, not the business of extracting, processing, and selling oil."

"Yeah, they call themselves energy companies now."

"And by focusing their attention on the problem, the need for energy, rather than what they do, which is produce and refine oil, they will be able to evolve by discovering and producing technologies and resources that will more effectively solve the energy problem than oil does."

"Oscar, you've really opened my eyes."

"That's why I'm here," he replies confidently. I watch him take another bite of his croissant and look up thoughtfully as he chews.

"Now, just a couple of fine points on this," he continues as he wipes his mouth with a napkin. "Your response to the question 'What do you do?' must be answered by a simple, one sentence response describing the solved problem. Your answer should be so simple a five-year-old can understand it and repeat it. Responses like 'I make prospects call you' or 'I make broken cars go' are simply stated concepts that trigger a person's curiosity. They're also easy for others to repeat. And that's the most important point."

"I don't understand."

"You can't expect your friend at the party to be able to articulate your business as accurately as you can. He or she isn't in your business. Therefore, the one sentence description has to be simple, easy to remember, and easy to repeat, like 'I make broken cars go.' Now, if you could coach the candlemaker on developing a one-line description of the problem he solved, a one-liner so simple a five-year-old could understand it and repeat it, what would you come up with?"

I scratch my chin in thought. "I've got one!" I exclaim. "If I were the candlemaker and were asked what I do, I would say, 'I cure the darkness.'"

"Beautiful!" Oscar bellows. "You could teach this stuff."

"You know, Oscar, it's such a simple concept that I could teach this."

"I'm glad to hear you say that, because in an upcoming lesson you'll learn that helping others to understand these ideas is an essential part of hanging out for a living."

~Your Crisis Has a Crisis~

Concerned, I clutch my teacup while I mull over the lesson I've just learned.

"What's on your mind, boy?"

"Oscar, you just made me realize I've got even bigger problems than I thought."

"Oh, how so?"

"Ten or fifteen years ago I could have said with all confidence that I make businesses easy to find, or I make your phone ring, or I cause prospects to call you. That all speaks to the problem advertising in the directory solves. But now I suddenly feel like I'm the one selling candles to cure the darkness."

"Explain," he says, picking up another croissant.

"Few people use the phone directories anymore. The ones who do are the holdouts that still don't have a computer. It's kind of like people in 1950s that still didn't have a phone, or those in the 1960s who didn't have a TV. They're few and far between, and their complete extinction is right around the corner.

"When a Yellow Page directory lands at my own doorstep, it never makes into the house. It goes right into the recycle bin. I can find any business in any category in any place with any solution to any problem I have with a few clicks," I say, holding up my smart phone. "In fact, this thing will even give me directions to the business I want to find right from where I'm sitting now. I can find what I'm looking for online in a fraction of the time it takes to look something up in the directory. Yellow Page USA is responding by pushing us to sell another product called Yellow Page Online along with directory ads. But even using their web page is just an extra step to getting to the search engine that you could just as easily go to directly."

"Hmm, sounds like you just found another crisis," Oscar says without the slightest hint of sympathy. "In fact"—a grin starts growing on his face— "sounds like your crisis has a crisis!" He lets out a guffaw and then bellows with laughter.

I stare at him, expressionless, seeing no humor in his comments.

"Lighten up, boy. What did you and I, just yesterday, agree that a crisis is in reality?" he asks enthusiastically.

"The wrapping of a gift that will lead to riches beyond my wildest dreams," I respond in monotone.

"Exactly. You should be delighted at the realization that your employer is a candlemaker before it's too late. Better than finding out with a proverbial pink slip of paper."

~Success Looks Like Luck (to Those Who Give Into Their Fears)~

"You know, Oscar, you're right. I guess I knew I was in a dying industry all along but was just afraid to see it because I'm in such a tough spot. I really need to make some money. I just don't know what to do."

"Yes you do. You're already doing it."

"I am? What?"

"That Sleazyfur Mutual thing."

"You mean Slarrefer. Well, yeah. But that's going to take some time. I can't jump into that yet."

"What?" Oscar barks, again leaning forward and looking me directly in the eye. "Let me get this straight. You're going to ignore the opportunity that you told me you believe is the answer to your financial struggles, the opportunity you believe others should participate in to get their financial house in order, the opportunity you spent $750 that you don't have on, the opportunity you put your marriage at risk over? Instead, you're going to continue to trade your time for money, always making just a little less than is necessary to get by, remaining in a perpetual state of just too busy and just too broke to pursue the dream of hanging out for a living? Maybe I got you wrong. Perhaps you're not ready to have me work with you."

He leans back, crosses his arms over his huge chest, and gives me a scowl that shows anger, disappointment, and frustration all at once. I feel like a child being scolded. Oscar's words send me back to a moment when I was five or six. I was at the edge of a day camp swimming pool, terrified of the water. An insensitive swimming instructor screamed at me to jump in and swim with the other kids.

"It's not that simple, Oscar. I'm afraid to go full-time with Slarrefer because I don't know when I would make enough money to survive. I'm on fumes as it is." I can feel my heart palpitating, and I begin to shake. Feeling ashamed that I may not be meeting Oscar's expectations of me, I avoid his stare by looking into my tea.

"Hey, do you trust your friend Oscar?" he says, again placing a reassuring hand on my shoulder.

"Sure I do." I look up to see his expression turn to empathy.

"The universe has a wonderful way of putting you in exactly the situation you need to be, in order for you to learn the lessons you must learn, for you to get to where you're going. You, my boy, are well on your way to great things. However, you must successfully complete this chapter of your journey before you can move on to the next. Understand, though, this is just a chapter."

"Embrace my circumstances?" I ask with a forced smile as I rub the mist from my eye with the back of my hand.

"Now you're thinking. Creation does not give any man a challenge that it doesn't also supply him with the ability to overcome. I wouldn't be here if I didn't believe you were destined for great things. This is the challenge of life. You can either embrace it or run from it."

"Life is like *Fear Factor*?"

"It's EXACTLY like *Fear Factor*," Oscar cheers, removing his hand from my shoulder. "I got news for you. Everyone else is in the same game, and they're just as scared as you. Successful people have discovered that success is largely a result of simply doing what everyone else is scared to do. Embrace the challenge of life, and you come to realize that what you fear is nothing more than shadows. You become emboldened to confront even more of life's challenges and, in so doing, reap even more rewards."

"Are you saying I should quit my job and go full-time with Slarrefer?"

"I said nothing of the sort," Oscar defends. "You do what you must to keep food on the table. But at the same time you must put some consistent effort into the vehicle that you really want to pursue. Do not forsake the fruits of tomorrow for the tribulations of today."

"I've heard this before, Oscar. It was a guy named Jim Rohn. He said, "Work full-time on your job and part-time on your fortune.""

"He was one of the greats of your time. Working full-time on your job and part-time on your fortune is very wise advice. And I suggest you follow it. Up 'til now all you've been doing is working full-time on your job and wondering about making a fortune instead of doing something about it."

I contemplate Oscar's words as I stare deeply into my cup of tea.

~Keep Portland Weird~

"Time to employ this morning's lesson. Today, go about your calls like always. When the subject of what you do comes up, answer with the problem you solve. I think you'll see a change in the way people talk to you."

"I already know I will," I reply enthusiastically.

Oscar stretches out, resting his arm on the backrest of the upholstered bench. "Now we still have much work to do. I'd like to join you in the field today if that's okay with you." He looks like he could easily rip a phone book in half and, yet, not walk very far without having to stop to catch his breath.

"You know, Oscar, I'd love the company, but . . . "

"Worried I'll get in your way?" he says, patting his belly.

"It's just that I have to move kind of quick, Oscar. I'm not sure you'll be able to keep up."

"Try me."

"I'm sure it's against company policy," I reply jokingly. "But I'd love to have you along . . . if you're up to it."

He returns my remark with the stare of a pool shark that has just found a patsy. "Where are we going today?"

"From the end of this block to the north end of the Pearl. I have to hit everything north of Hoyt between Ninth and Thirteenth."

"Wonderful! While we're walking, we can discuss our next lesson."

"What is our next lesson?" I ask, gathering up my belongings.

"Today you'll discover how to attract business by taking a greater interest in other peoples' business than you have in promoting your own."

"I can't wait!"

I realize I've hardly touched my tea as I stand to leave. Hurriedly, I take a gulp and am painfully surprised to find it's still piping hot, scalding the roof of my mouth.

"Easy, boy. What's your rush?"

I fan my mouth with my hand. "Oscar, I have to get to work. I have to bring a business card from each business I visit back to the office this afternoon along with the name of a decision maker or some other evidence that I was actually there. If I don't at least show them I'm hitting these businesses, they'll for sure can me before my ninety days are up."

"Well . . . I wouldn't want to hold you up," he says sitting comfortably, clearly in no rush to leave the table.

"You can finish the tea if you want while I go pay the check."

"That's very kind of you."

I gather up my belongings and make my way out to the front counter where Janie is busily sorting through some paperwork. "I need to get going, Janie. What do I owe you?"

She looks at me with a surprised expression. "Is everything okay?"

"Yeah. I loved that stuff. My friend's going to finish the pot," I tell her as I pull the wallet from my back pocket.

"Are you all right?" she asks with concern.

"Yeah. Why? What's wrong?"

"Tyler, I took that pot back to you less than a minute ago. There's no one else back there."

I wonder if she's crazy or just pulling my leg. "I've been back there for at least an hour. I got here at nine," I reply as I pull out my smart phone, which also serves as my primary way of keeping time. I stare at it with astonishment. It reads 9:01 a.m. "Oh," I say under my breath, feeling both confused and embarrassed. "Umm . . . hold on just one second." I place my briefcase on the floor against the foot of the counter, run to the entrance of the lounge, and look around. It's empty. My pot of tea is still sitting on the table. "He did it to me again," I say under my breath as I return to the counter while trying to come up with a graceful way of explaining myself. "You know, I guess I just have a lot on my mind," I say with an uncomfortable laugh, not knowing how I'm going to finish the conversation. "If it seems like I might be a nut, you know, in a harmless sort of way, can I still be a customer?"

She shakes her head back and forth as she prints out the receipt. "Hey, man, I'm cool with it. If it weren't for the likes of you, we'd be out of business," she says, pointing to a bumper sticker adhered to the side of the cash register that reads "Keep Portland Weird."

I pay and leave as quickly as I can.

Be the solution to a problem, not a "doer" of my Job.

What would someone overhear at a party that would prompt them to suggest that the person doing the complaining should contact me for a solution?
  (The business line doesn't ring enough)

A one-sentence description of the problem I solve and how. So simple a 5-year-old can understand it and repeat it.

- I cause businesses to get calls from qualified prospects.

- I make business lines ring.

          Don't be a candlemaker!

PART TWO

FIVE

It's All About Relationships

I walk out of the Tea Zone into the muggy summer air, reeling from the disorientation of having spent an hour with Oscar that has turned out to be no more than a minute. The smell of diesel exhaust from a passing truck hangs thick over the street, prompting me to momentarily hold my breath as I quickly walk toward the Saturn. Emerging from the cloud of fumes, I exhale with a loud gasp and look up to see a familiar portly figure filing his nails, leaning against the passenger door of my car. As I get closer, part of me wants to run up and give him a hug just for being there, another wants to run screaming in the opposite direction to avoid facing the absurd dream that's following me. I walk up to the car, put the key in the lock of the trunk, and give my unlikely mentor a stare accompanied by a flustered sigh. I just want to let him know that I'm annoyed at being ditched and left with the impossible task of explaining myself at the Tea Zone.

"What's wrong, boy? You said I could join you in the field," he remarks while briefly looking up at me with one eye while continuing to groom his nails. "And you were worried I wouldn't be able to keep up. Ha!"

Rather than respond I open the trunk and pull out my sample directory and presentation binder.

"What are you doing with all that junk?" he growls.

"It's my sales materials. I need this stuff to show people the book."

"Not today you don't. Put that crap back in your car."

I open my mouth to object but stop myself, deciding to instead conserve my mental energy. No point getting into an unwinnable argument with an opponent who outclasses me in more ways than I can probably imagine. I return the items to the trunk, pick up my briefcase, and look at him shaking his head back and forth, signaling to me that it won't be coming either.

"That's better," he says over the sound of the trunk slamming closed. Oscar has this mischievous, ornery side that is at some moments endearing, and at others exasperating. I don't know why, but it makes him kind of lovable. He motions for me to join him as he turns and walks ahead. "Let's get going."

I'm struck by how easily he carries his rotund physique as we start up the sidewalk. "Going to be another warm one," he declares, pulling a white handkerchief from his pocket to wipe his brow. Our path leads us under a canopy of young maples lining the street. The intense sun, filtered by the broad foliage above us, casts a surreal emerald green hue along our path.

"I suppose you're wondering why I had you leave your sales stuff in the car?"

"It crossed my mind."

"In order to hang out for a living, you're going to have to develop the habit of taking a greater interest in others' business than you have in promoting your own."

"You said that in the Tea Zone. So what does that have to do with my bringing presentation materials on my route?"

~Gardening Versus Hunting~

"Remember the example of our friend Bob at the business mixer?"

"Yeah."

"Well, imagine this time he turns to you and says, 'Hi. I'm Bob, the mechanic. I own Bob's repair shop. We fix both domestic and foreign cars. If you ever need any repair work, don't hesitate to give me a call. Here's my card.' He hands you his card and turns to another person, extends his hand, and repeats what he said to you word for word."

"Oscar, that's what people do at networking events." I answer as we walk, brushing away a fly. "He's just working the room to get his name out there."

"How does it make you feel when people do that?"

I ponder the question. "When people do that, it tells me that I'm just a number to them. But it also makes me feel like prey. Like they're just sniffing me to see if I might taste good. It's obvious people like that don't give a damn about me unless they can sell me something. Unless I saw him as a potential client, I'd probably toss his card when I got home."

"In other words, you would have no interest in Bob or his business."

"Probably not."

"Now think about this question carefully before you answer. Did Bob do anything wrong? Was his behavior immoral, unethical, or illegal?"

"Well, no. It's just self-serving, bordering on rude."

"Why?"

"Because he's only interested in talking about himself to serve his own agenda."

"So Bob wasn't doing anything wrong? He was just being ineffective?"

"Let's just say he wouldn't get me as a client with that approach."

Oscar continues. "Now imagine the same scenario. You're at the business mixer, and this time Bob approaches you and simply says, 'Hi, I'm Bob.' What would be your response?"

"I guess I'd say, 'Hi, I'm Tyler.'"

"And Bob responds, 'What do you do, Tyler?'"

"I help businesses get calls from qualified prospects."

"And Bob says, 'Really? I'd like to know more about how you do that. Can I get your card?'"

"I'd gladly give him one."

"Of course you would. And Bob looks at your card and says, 'Hmm . . . Yellow Page USA. How long have you been with them?'"

"I just started a couple of months ago."

"And to that Bob asks, 'Would you be open to getting together for coffee so we can find out about each other's businesses?'"

"I'd say, 'Sure. Can I get your card?'"

Oscar raises his hand, signaling to me that I can stop the role-playing. "Which Bob did you prefer in this exercise?"

"The second one, by a long shot."

"Why?"

"Because he was interested in me. He made me feel important, like he cared. The first Bob was only interested in promoting himself."

"So you preferred the second example because the person in that example was interested in you and made you feel important. The first example did not appeal to you because the person was interested only in himself and his agenda. And, as you put it, the result was that you felt like prey."

"I'd say that pretty well sums it up."

"And yet here you are, prepared to use the first Bob's approach on today's sales route: going door-to-door hunting for customers, carrying a bunch of sales materials, and spewing a sales pitch that only serves *your* agenda."

Oscar's analogy gives me an eye-opening and very uncomfortable perspective. "I never saw myself like that. You really think I've been coming off that way to people?"

"Never having been the recipient of one of your cold calls, I can't say. Perhaps your results answer that question better than I can."

Now feeling horrible about myself, I just stare at the sidewalk in front of us as we walk.

"Hey, don't go gettin' yourself in a funk over it," Oscar says, placing a reassuring hand on my shoulder. "At least now you understand why it's more important to take a greater interest in the other person's business than it is to promote your own. Your earlier use of the word *prey* was quite apropos. Try this analogy: Bob number one was hunting. Bob number two was gardening."

"I get what you mean about hunting. But what do you mean by gardening?"

"We're going to use gardening as a metaphor throughout our lessons because it applies perfectly to hanging out for a living. Building productive and fulfilling business relationships is very much like planting a garden. It takes more time, but the eventual harvest is well worth it."

"I'm still not following you."

~The Cantaloupe Patch~

"Ever plant a vegetable garden?"

"Yeah. When I was around thirteen I grew cantaloupe in my mother's yard."

"Were you successful at growing cantaloupe?"

"Once I got the hang of it. My first try ended with a pretty crummy harvest. But after a couple of more tries, I learned what to do, and I was growing the best cantaloupe on Earth. One year I had so many I couldn't give them away fast enough."

"What is the first thing you need to grow cantaloupe?"

"Cantaloupe seeds, I guess."

"And what's required to turn cantaloupe seeds into cantaloupe?"

"The basic ingredients are nutrient rich soil, enough water, and plenty of sun. When you're thirteen, a little patience is helpful too."

Oscar chuckles. "I get the idea. So according to you, one must nurture the seeds and allow the vine to produce fruit in its own time before one can enjoy a harvest."

"Of course."

"Now I have a few more questions for you."

"Shoot."

"What did you expect from the cantaloupe seeds?"

"Cantaloupe."

"Did all of the seeds you planted produce cantaloupe?"

"No, in fact, most of the seeds either didn't come up or they died. Doesn't really matter, though. Only takes a couple of healthy vines to get a ton of cantaloupe."

"So you planted lots of seeds?"

"Yeah, you have to. They don't all grow."

"Did you treat the seeds that grew any differently than the ones that didn't?"

"Of course not. Some grow, some don't. What does all this have to do with hanging out for a living?" I ask impatiently as we stroll toward the sound of children playing in the park at Jameson Square.

"Imagine growing cantaloupe the way you have been attempting to grow your business," he says, removing his hand from my shoulder so he can wave both hands about. "It's a little like showing up at planting time with a shotgun rather than a shovel. One must grow cantaloupes, not hunt them. In order to hang out for a living, you're going to have to think of customers as fruit of the vine, rather than prey to be hunted.

"As of today, I want you to see each person as a seed with unknown possibilities. In order to discover the potential in the seed, you must nurture the relationship and allow it to grow and bloom." The large man momentarily grows quiet as we walk past the south end of the park, and then gives me a pat on the back as he finishes his thought. "However, just like cantaloupe, not all business relationships grow. But, like you said, it takes only a couple of vines to give you a bigger harvest than you know what to do with."

As we pass Jameson Square, the mist from the fountain drifts into our path, cooling the air. I stop in the middle of the sidewalk as Oscar continues walking. "But Oscar, I don't have time to grow relationships like cantaloupe. I need to eat now. It takes a good three or four months to produce cantaloupe from seed. I bet business relationships take even longer," I protest over the sound of splashing water and the screams of kids playing in the park.

He stops, turns around, and shoots me a stern look. "I got some bad news for you, boy. Four months from now is going to come, no matter what. You need to stop thinking like Bob number one and start thinking like Bob number two. Imagine a farmer staring at bags of seed at planting time saying, 'I don't have time to grow this stuff; I need food now.'" He then turns away to continue ahead without me. "Your circumstances six months from now will be determined entirely upon what you do today, just as your current circumstances are the result of choices you made six months, a year, even two years ago," he shouts from up ahead.

He continues on as I stand still on the sidewalk, momentarily befuddled by the conflict I'm having between his analogy and the reality that I only have twenty-nine days to hit my revenue quota.

"Based on the results you've gotten so far, where do you suppose you'll be in five or six months if you keep on hunting for clients?" he yells, his voice growing more distant as he keeps moving forward.

I start after him, shouting back. "Right where I am now, probably worse. But I've been doing my job exactly the way they taught me in training."

~Forrest Gump~

Just as I catch up, Oscar stops at a sidewalk cafe just opening for business and gestures for me to take a seat as he pulls a chair out from a table shaded by a large umbrella. "Take a load off, kid. We got plenty of time. I need to remind you of something." As we both settle in at the table, Oscar leans back with a stretch, props his sandaled feet up on an empty chair, and places his hands behind his head, revealing his huge belly under a shirt held only partially closed by one button at the naval.

"Your purpose, as you shared it with me, is to build your financial service enterprise. That enterprise is, by design, promoted through word-of-mouth. It's not possible to build a sustainable word-of-mouth organization by selling people a product or an opportunity, and the reason is simple: less than ten percent of the population is wired to sell in the transactional sense. But," he says with a dramatic pause, "*everyone* is wired to share. In order for a network marketing organization to grow and thrive, it must be shared using a simple method duplicable to the lowest level of competency. Our formula for hanging out requires the same level of competency as third grade show and tell. Yes, it takes time, but it's effective, sustainable, and when applied to a direct marketing venture, becomes self-perpetuating. Let's return to your more immediate concern, which is how this applies to your sales job."

He stares into the bright turquoise sky with a distant gaze while he gathers his thoughts. After several moments, he lets out a loud sigh, and continues the conversation. "A brilliant physicist by the name of Albert Einstein once said, 'Everyone's a genius. But if you judge a fish by it's ability to climb a tree, it will live its whole life believing it is stupid.' Your company taught you to do your job by hunting, which is a great sales model for your company, but not for you. It's just not your nature. A man who lives in conflict with his nature is a most unhappy man indeed. Your struggle to perform your job isn't a sign of incompetence; it's a reflection of the conflict between your company's sales process and how you happen to be wired. I believe the rest of today's lesson will help you with that dilemma."

He looks over at me. "Ever told someone about a movie that you really enjoyed?"

"Sure. I remember that, after seeing *Forrest Gump* the first time, I watched it five more times because I took five different friends to see it. I love that movie!"

"Why did you take those people to see Forrest Gump?"

"Because I enjoyed it, and I thought my friends would too."

"What did you expect in return from those people?"

"I didn't expect anything in return. They're my friends. I wanted to share a good movie with them. That's what friends do."

"Do you recall what preceded the invitation to see *Forrest Gump* with you?"

"I don't understand. What do you mean by 'what preceded the invitation'?"

"Did you ever have any contact with the people you invited to the movie prior to actually inviting them?"

"Of course. They were my friends."

"So a friendship preceded the invitation," he confirms.

"Well . . . yes, of course. I wouldn't call a stranger and invite them to the movies."

"You wouldn't?" he answers sarcastically. "Then why would you invite a stranger to hear a pitch about your directory?"

Straining to come up with an answer, I blurt out, "It's my job."

"What do you mean?"

"Oscar, I get paid to show people the directory."

"So let me get this straight. It would be inappropriate to invite a stranger to the movies, but it's okay to invite a stranger to see your directory presentation because it's your job?"

Recognizing the implied hypocrisy illustrated by Oscar's question, I struggle to reply. "I think you just lost me again, Oscar. Taking friends to the movies and doing business are two different things."

"Not when you hang out for a living they're not." Removing his hands from behind his head and his feet from the chair, Oscar leans forward to look me dead in the eye. "Think about it. Of the eleven people you invited to go see *Forest Gump*, how many accepted the invitation?"

"All of them."

"And how many people did you invite to see your Yellow Page presentation last week?"

"Almost a hundred, I guess."

"And how many of those accepted your invitation?"

"Just seven so far. But I have to follow up."

"How much follow-up did you have to do when you invited your friends to the movies?"

"None."

"So explain to me why in one case you have one hundred percent success without any need for follow-up, and in the other you have almost no success."

"It's the relationship, Oscar. I have a relationship with my friends. I don't have one with the people I cold-call on."

"Exactly!" he exclaims, slamming an open palm down on the table, almost startling me out of my chair. "And *that* is the difference, the relationship. Hanging out for a living is all about relationships."

Oscar leans back, again folding his hands behind his head and closing his eyes, leaving me startled and still not completely understanding. I hate it when he does this. Am I supposed to ask a question? Do I stay silent so he can concentrate? Did he just fall asleep on me? The idea of giving him a poke to see if he's still with me crosses my mind just as he reopens his eyes and stares blankly into the sky.

"Let's look at this a little differently," he continues. "What do you hope to accomplish today by visiting businesses on your sales route?"

"Well . . . ultimately, to make some sales."

"So you want to make some sales?" he responds at half-speed.

"I think that's what I just said."

"So how many of these businesses that you're going to visit do you intend to buy something from?"

"What do you mean? I don't want to buy anything, Oscar. I'm there to sell."

"Fair enough. Now these businesses that you're going to visit, what do they want?"

"More business?"

"Very good. And how many of them do you suppose opened their doors this morning with the intention of buying something from a walk-in salesperson?"

It takes me a second to process the question. "I guess none."

"So if you were in the shoes of the people you intend to visit today, how would you feel about a guy stopping in to sell Yellow Page advertising?"

"Annoyed, just like I felt when you described Bob number one," I reply with a deflated sigh.

"So you're not there to buy anything, and they're not there to buy anything. You're both there to sell something. Doesn't sound like the beginning of a very successful relationship, does it?" he says, continuing to look into the sky.

"No, it doesn't," I reply. Oscar has now brought me to the bottom of the canyon. I'll feel like the scum of the Earth if I continue doing my job the way I have been, but I still have no idea how to do it any differently. I place an elbow on the table, rest my cheek in the palm of my hand, and cock my head toward him. "I hope there's more to this, Oscar, 'cause right now you've got me feeling pretty lousy about working my route today."

"No reason to feel lousy. All we've done is agree that what you want and what your prospects want is the same thing: to generate some revenue and to interact with people who are more interested in you than they are in selling you something. Here's my point. You're a good person, and your very presence can enrich others' lives. All you have to do is allow them to discover that. Then they'll become curious to learn about your business."

With my self-esteem in tatters, I'm having a hard time accepting Oscar's assessment that I'm a good person. "So how do I allow people to find out what a great guy I am?" I ask sarcastically.

"By being yourself." He gives me a worried look and then a gentle slap on the cheek to snap me out of my momentary self-pity. "Hey, this is where I need you to trust me, because this is so simple you may have trouble believing it. This morning, I want you to visit the businesses on your assigned route just like always. But instead of selling to them, learn about them. Find out what they do and what they want. You'll discover that by being interested in others you'll become a very interesting person to them."

I don't understand what Oscar's talking about and return an empty stare to let him know it. He taps a fingernail on the white metal table to get me to listen closely. "Until you experience the result of promoting who you are rather than what you do, this will all just be theory for you. So it's time for the acid test. As you walk your territory this morning, just build relationships instead of trying to sell Yellow Page ads."

"And how do I do that?"

~A Different Approach~

"As you enter each business, ask for nothing except a business card. I assure you, all will be happy to give you one. Then introduce yourself, explain that you're expanding your business into the neighborhood, and that you just wanted to stop by to see if you can schedule a time to find out more about them and their business."

"But Oscar, that's what's gotten me tossed out of almost every business I've walked into over the last two months," I protest.

"No, trying to sell advertising to the wrong people is what's gotten you thrown out," he replies, sounding annoyed. "Now look, as long as you have to cold-call on these businesses, you might as well use it as an opportunity to learn today's lesson. Do you remember what that is?" he says in a rather condescending tone.

"Take a greater interest in others' business than I have in promoting my own," I answer sheepishly, feeling like a scolded child.

"Right. So let me connect the dots for you. First, ask for a card. Second, introduce yourself. Third, invite them to hang out so you can learn about each other. That's it. Just walk in, introduce yourself, and get a card. But instead of trying to set an appointment to show them the phone directory, you're going to invite them to coffee. Don't worry about using the right words. Come from your heart, not your head. Just like you were introducing yourself to a new neighbor and then inviting them over for tea. In this case, you're going to invite them to hang out."

"I get it, Oscar, but it's a hard idea to get used to. I've been doing things my way for so long I guess it's just gotten to be a habit, even though it doesn't work."

"Granted, it's a paradigm shift. Think of it like getting used to a new pair of glasses. It's a little awkward at first, but by wearing them the shift occurs quite naturally. After actively putting our lessons into practice today, you won't be able to imagine doing your job the way you did it just yesterday."

"Sounds too easy," I respond doubtfully as I push my chair back and stand to leave. "You know, Oscar, if it were anyone else telling me this, I wouldn't believe it. But if I can believe you exist and I'm talking to you, I guess I can believe anything."

"Wonderful! Where do we start?"

I point to a small medical supply store across the street. "That place right there."

"Time to get to work. Now scoot," he says, waving his hands to shoo me away.

"Okay, here goes."

I walk across the street to the small storefront. As I approach, I can see a young woman through the window sitting at a desk. What appears to be an older gentleman is pacing around, talking on the phone. "I can do this. I can do my job by hanging out. I'm going to offer to hang out with these people," I tell myself unconvincingly as I reach the small shop.

The noise of the bell that hangs on the door startles me as I enter. The young woman looks up. "Good morning," she greets me with a thick accent. The gentleman on the phone, who appears to be in his early seventies, is speaking with a very deep, gravelly voice in what sounds like Russian.

"I hope I'm not interrupting."

"Not at all. How can we help you?" she replies with a tone that seems to get cheerier with each word.

"I was wondering if I could get a card?"

"Of course," she replies, handing me a card from the business card holder on her desk. "Is there anything we can do for you?"

I'm momentarily struck by the question. No one had ever asked me that when I walked in carrying all of my sales materials.

"I'm Tyler. I just stopped by to introduce myself. I'm expanding my business into the neighborhood and was hoping to find out more about your business, and see if there's a way we might network with each other."

The man finishes his call and walks over to me. "I am Anton. This is my daughter, Nadia. What is your business?" he asks in his thick accent.

"Nice to meet you both. I'm with . . . " I catch myself. I was about to say the name of the company, but I remember what Oscar taught me: answer with the solution to the problem you solve. "I help businesses get calls from qualified prospects," I reply confidently. "And what about you? Looks like you offer a pretty wide selection of medical supplies."

"Yes, this is the showroom," Nadia answers.

"How do you make businesses get calls?" Anton asks.

"With the Yellow Page USA directory."

"We don't need no stinking yellow pages," Anton growls, arrogantly dismissing me by waving me away with one hand.

"And I don't need any medical supplies. I just wanted to meet you. You know, in my job, I visit businesses all day long. If you'd be open to setting a time to get together to tell me about your business, and whom I can refer your way, I bet I'd come across some other business owners that could use your service. And, if you want, I'd be happy to share with you the kind of advertisers I'm looking for. You know, just network."

"Of course!" replies Nadia. "We would love to network."

Anton looks at Nadia and nods his head in agreement.

"When would you like to meet?" Nadia asks.

"I could come by Thursday morning. Would ten o'clock be okay?"

Anton looks at his daughter, who gives him an enthusiastic nod.

"Great!" I exclaim. "I'll give you a call before then, just to confirm."

"You have card?" Anton asks.

"Oh, of course," I say, reaching into my pocket to hand a card to each of them.

"Very nice to meet you, TylerTy-ler," Anton says as he looks at my card.

"Nice to meet you too, Anton, Nadia," I answer with a tip of my head. "Have a great day!"

I stop on the sidewalk outside the store, write *Coffee—10:00—Thurs* on the back of Nadia's business card, and reflect upon what has just happened. I scheduled an appointment to meet with new friends to discuss how we could help each other, not an appointment to try to sell an ad. *Corporate sure wouldn't like this approach. But so what? They're going to fire me anyway,* I think with a shrug. Looking across the street, I see Oscar still reclined on the two chairs under the sidewalk umbrella. I give a thumbs-up, and he nods back.

Over the next couple of hours, I use the same approach with each business that I visit. Some still ask me what I'm selling, but nearly half of the people I talk to want to get together to chat about how we can refer business to each other. By the time I complete my route, I've gathered nearly twenty cards from people who want to get together so we can learn about each other's business.

Six

The Egg, the Goose,
and the Granny Goose

It's almost noon by the time I return to the sidewalk cafe to find Oscar eating something from a small dish.

"Oh . . . this is wonderful! It's called gelato," he exclaims as I approach the table.

"No, *this* is wonderful!" I respond with glee, taking a seat across from him and plopping a stack of business cards on the table. "Oscar, I set six appointments to hang out, and eight people want me to call them to set up an appointment! And it was so easy! Like introducing myself to new neighbors, just like you said."

Oscar nods in acknowledgement as he shovels another spoonful into his mouth, obviously more interested in his icy treat than the results of my neighborhood walk. As I look through the cards and the notes I made on them, I realize that I've made enough connections to book appointments out for the next week. It's the first time since I started with Yellow Page USA that I feel good about my work. Oscar places his empty dish on the table and slides a menu over to me. "You must be hungry."

"Hungry and hot," I answer, turning to look inside the air-conditioned cafe. Not a single empty seat. "Looks like we're stuck out here."

"It's not so bad," Oscar replies, perspiration running from his forehead down to his cheek as he dabs his face with a handkerchief. "This is nothing compared to a July day back in old Mesopotamia."

His comment reminds me that none of this can be real. Oscar's presence alone is enough to convince me that I've left reality as I know it, but the whole world seems slightly out of phase, like an old photograph with a sort of a sepia patina to it. The smell of wet cement from a neighboring shopkeeper hosing down the sidewalk makes the already muggy air feel even stickier. A smoky, accordion version of "Begin the Beguine" plays in the background giving a sort of European ambiance to the moment.

Since the moment I felt that tingling sensation from the teapot yesterday, it seems like I've been in some kind of strange dream, but hunger distracts me from dwelling too long on the notion that I'm trapped in an alternate universe.

Famished, I pick up the menu to look it over. The prices take my breath away. I'm in no position to buy myself lunch. I'd planned on eating the sandwich and tangerine that Karen prepared for me last night, this time safely chilled in a small Styrofoam cooler in the car. *How do I tell Oscar I can't afford lunch?* I think with a gulp as I hide behind the menu.

Unsure of how to explain my awkward situation, I look up from the menu to see Oscar looking directly at me with an expression that says he understands.

"Lunch is on me, kid. Order anything you want."

"You don't have to do that, Oscar," I say reflexively.

"It's my pleasure." He looks over his shoulder and waves his hand at the cafe window.

"Thanks!" I respond, returning my attention to the menu. It seems like it's been so long since I've had a meal that didn't come out of a can or box that I'm actually a bit intimidated by the eclectic assortment of mouth-watering French and Italian inspired dishes. An item toward the top catches my eye.

-*Arugula Chicken Salad*-
Crispy Prosciutto, Candied Walnuts, and Goat Cheese
with Fig Vinaigrette.

It sounds both healthy and delicious. I lay the menu on the table and return my attention to Oscar in anticipation of continuing the conversation. A moment later a gentleman arrives at our table with a pitcher of ice water and a pair of glasses. "How was the gelato, Oscar?" he asks.

"It was wonderful, Sid. Perfect for a day like today. Sid, this is Tyler. He'll be joining me for lunch."

"Very good. Can I get you fellas something to drink?"

"Can I get an Arnold Palmer?" I ask.

"Sure thing."

"Make it two," Oscar chimes in.

"Coming up. I'll be back in a minute to take your orders."

Until now, I've been doing a pretty good job of playing along with the utter weirdness of it all, but as Sid walks back into the café, I have to mention the obvious. "Oscar, he can see you!"

"Of course he can see me. What, you think he's hard of seein'?"

"But nobody at the Tea Zone saw you."

"Obviously they weren't lookin' very close!" he grins, patting his stomach with both hands. "Now what do you say we proceed with our lesson?" he continues, quickly changing the subject and leaving me somewhat bewildered.

~A Simple Formula~

"As I told you yesterday, hanging out for a living requires mastering the art of attracting business by referral. Today I'm going to give you a simple formula that will completely change how you go about developing business relationships."

He stares at me with an intense expression, hand on his chin, tapping his lips with his index finger. "Ever try to follow a recipe but the dish didn't come out so well?"

I think back to the Valentine's Day disaster when I thought it would be a good idea to fix Karen a special dinner. "I sure have."

"Did you follow a recipe?"

"Actually, I did. Very carefully, I thought."

"Then why didn't the meal come out as expected? Was there something wrong with the recipe?"

"No, I think there was something wrong with the cook," I chuckle while loosening my collar and rolling up my shirt sleeves, trying to get a little more comfortable in the sticky noon air.

"Oh, and what was wrong with the cook?"

"He didn't know how to cook!"

We both let out a laugh as Sid returns with our drinks and a plate of unusual looking hors d'oeuvres. "Here's a little something, compliments of the house."

"What is it?" I ask, not sure I can trust the strange looking, round objects.

"Fried green olives stuffed with smoked mozzarella. Careful, they're still hot," he cautions while removing an order pad from an apron pocket and a pencil from behind his ear. "So you fellas decide what you want?"

Oscar pulls a pair of glasses from his shirt pocket and gestures for me to go ahead while he reads the menu.

"I'd like a large arugula chicken salad," I answer, while sniffing an olive at the end of my fork.

"Excellent choice. How about you, Oscar?"

"How's the salmon, Sid?" he asks, peering over his glasses.

"Just came in this morning, Oscar. It's a wild caught spring chinook. It was pan roasted a little more than an hour ago, then chilled. On hot days like today, it's served cold with dill-crushed red potatoes and asparagus topped with a gribiche sauce."

"That ought to hit the spot," Oscar replies, handing the menu back to Sid.

"I'll be back in a bit with your orders. Enjoy the olives."

For a split second it strikes me as odd that a 2,500-year-old guy who lives in a teapot and surfs through curved space-time would need reading glasses, but the smell of the unusual appetizer makes my stomach growl, redirecting my attention to the olives. I hesitantly eat one and give Oscar an expression of approval, letting him know that they're safe. He pops one in his mouth and chews with a thoughtful look, making me wonder if he's contemplating the olive or what he's going to say next.

"Learning the formula for building a referral based business," he swallows and continues, "is a bit like learning to cook. It's not complicated, but until you have just a little experience, it's easy to screw up. The real danger is that, just like the failed recipe, it can appear you're doing everything right, even though you're not. When you don't get the desired result, the natural assumption would be that the formula doesn't work. Therefore, in addition to your lessons, I'll have you put the formula into practice in the field to make sure you are gettin' the desired result.

"Now, hanging out for a living involves creating strategic business alliances with the right people. We'll call them your target market. We're going to start with a tactical brainstorming process designed to identify target markets."

"I'm all ears."

"Identifying target markets is the single most important part of the mechanics of hanging out for a living. You might, in fact, be able to hang out for a living with an understanding of just this one principle, even without the rest of our lessons—provided, of course, that you have the philosophy of servitude," he says pointing his finger at me to emphasize the point.

"There are three steps to identifying your target market, and it's vital that you thoroughly comprehend each one. The first step is to make up an ideal client."

"That's easy for me, Oscar. My ideal client is anyone who wants to advertise in the Yellow Page directory."

I watch his face go deadpan. In a sarcastic gesture, he places his elbows on the table and buries his face in his hands.

"No good?" I ask sheepishly.

He looks up, reaches over the small table, and pinches my cheek with one hand while gently slapping the other. "Sweet kid . . . I've really got my work cut out for me." With a loud sigh, he leans back and folds his hands on his stomach.

"Time for a couple of rules. First, your ideal client isn't an *anyone* or a *someone*. It's a well-defined description of whom you seek to serve. Second, your target market it *not* your ideal client. Your target market is that person or entity who has a network of people who have a network of people whom you seek to serve."

I try repeating Oscar's last statement, hoping that by doing so it will make some sense to me. "My target market is the entity that has a network that have people—"

Oscar cuts me off. "Don't worry about it. By the time we're finished with lunch, you'll understand completely. Write this down," he says wiggling a finger at my pad of paper. "Ideal clients must be invented, not sought."

~The Story of Aladdin~

As I finish writing, Oscar asks, "You ever hear the ancient folk story of Aladdin and the magic lamp?"

"Yeah, but I don't think I've heard it since I was a little kid."

"Tell me what you remember," he says, reaching for another olive. He savors the morsel, settles into the molded plastic chair, and closes his eyes.

"Something about a boy in the Middle or Far East," I begin, "or someplace like that, who found an old oil lamp. When he rubbed the lamp to shine it up, a genie appeared and. . . ."

I stop myself as the parallels between the story I'm recalling and my experience with Oscar begin to dawn on me. "Oscar, are you?"

With eyes still closed, he waves his hand dismissing my obvious conclusion. "No relation whatsoever. Continue."

I do a double take at Oscar before attempting to continue my recollection of the story, wrestling with the unavoidable similarities. "Okay, well, the genie told Aladdin he would grant him three wishes. I'm not sure how the story ended, but I seem to remember things didn't go well." I struggle to recall the ending. "It was like . . . well, when Aladdin was granted his first two wishes, there were unintended consequences, and the last wish was to undo the first two, or something like that. That's about all I remember." I shrug my shoulders and reach for another olive.

"Over the centuries," Oscar begins as he slowly opens his eyes, "the story of the lamp has taken many forms. The story is a metaphor, which is often used to convey a specific lesson. One common theme is to be careful what you ask for, lest you attain it.

"In my time, there was a version of the story which was about a beggar who inadvertently came into possession of the lamp. When the beggar called forth its power, a djinni, or genie, as you say, appeared and announced, 'What wouldst thou with me? I am the slave of the lamp and will obey thee in all things thrice.' Without a moment's thought, the beggar shouted his reply. 'I wish for treasure: gold, silver and precious stones. More than any man has ever possessed.' With a voice that filled the air like thunder, the djinni proclaimed 'And so it is. Behold!' With a loud rumble, the ground quaked, and a mound of treasure standing taller than any structure in the village materialized before the beggar."

I don't know when I've been so entertained. Oscar is a master spellbinder. He has me absolutely captivated, not as much by the story as his telling of it, with the eloquence and animation of a Shakespearean actor.

"Within moments," he continues, "Several grimy-faced children descend upon the treasure with glee, like ants at a picnic. 'This will not do!' The beggar cries to the djinni. 'My treasure will surely be pilfered in no time! You must make it absolutely safe so that no one, but I, may have access to it.'

"'*And so it is,*' The djinni roars.

"In an instant the beggar finds himself alone in a large cavern with his treasure, and this pleases him very much. Consumed by his good fortune, he spends the next several hours sorting his riches: diamonds in one pile, rubies in another, gold coins in yet another, and so forth. Eventually he grows tired and hungry. The realization that he can now afford to dine like the kings and emperors makes his mouth water. After filling his pockets with several coins, he searches for the exit to the cavern. Unable to find it, he summons the djinni a third time and asks, 'Where is the entrance to this place so that I may leave to enjoy my first meal as a wealthy man?'

"'There is no entrance or exit to this safest of places,' replies the djinni. 'In accordance with your last command, your treasure has been made absolutely safe. Only you have access to it. Therefore there is no way in or out of the cavern.'

"'But I will starve!' cries the beggar. 'What good is the treasure if I am unable to come and go as I please in order to enjoy it?'

"'Dost thou desire to make your third wish?' The djinni asks.

"The beggar now realizes that he must be very careful in how he words his third wish," Oscar says, again wagging his index finger at me. With that he leans back and, as if someone has flipped a switch, closes his eyes and seems to go into a deep meditation.

I sit for a moment, waiting for more. "Is that it?"

With his eyes still closed, Oscar replies, "Pretty much."

"So the moral of the story is, 'Be careful what you ask for'?"

"Precisely."

He remains silent for several moments. Then, as if coming out of a trance, he gradually opens his eyes and reaches for another olive. "Now let's see how much you've learned from the experience of our friend, the beggar." He eats the olive, wipes his hand with a napkin, and picks up a dribble-spouted bottle of olive oil from the table.

"Imagine a genie emerged from this bottle and offered to grant you an endless source of your ideal client. Now genies, by their nature, aren't very bright. They don't have the ability to give you what you want. They can only give you *exactly* what you ask for. In other words, what you describe is exactly what you get. Therefore, it would be a good idea to describe a person or entity that you would particularly enjoy working with. Who would you *love* to have as a client? Don't limit yourself to what you think is possible. Use your imagination. You have the power of the lamp," he says, holding the bottle of olive oil up to my face. "What do you ask for?"

In an overly dramatic gesture to make his point, Oscar returns the bottle to the table, lays down his fork, holds up a closed fist, and begins prying it open, one finger at a time. "What industry are they in? Do they have a problem you enjoy solving? Are they the kind of people you would want to spend time with, regardless of the business relationship? Can they afford your service? Where are they located?" Running out of fingers, he continues gesturing with both hands. "Are they male or female? Single or a couple? Sole proprietor or a corporation? Are they looking for your service right now? Think about what attributes you can give this client that would make them ideal for you. Have fun with it. There are no limitations. You get to make it up. Just remember, the genie hasn't the ability to give you what you want. The genie can only give you what is asked for. So think before you ask, and be very specific. Let's start with your description of the person or entity that you wish to have purchase an advertisement in your directory. Once you've gotten the entire formula, we'll apply it to that Slippery Mutual thing."

"It's Slarrefer!" I snap back, thoroughly annoyed at his continued mispronunciation of the company name.

"Isn't that what I said?" Oscar replies innocently.

Sid returns, interrupting our conversation as he sets our lunch plates on the table. "I'll be back in a minute to refill your glasses. You guys need anything else?" We both shake our heads. "Enjoy your lunch fellas . . . and you listen to your dad," Sid says, pointing to me as he leaves.

"Ha!" Oscar lets out his familiar, boisterous laugh, amused at Sid's misinterpretation of our relationship. I shake my head and dig into my salad. "Enjoy your lunch, kid," Oscar says with a giggle. He plunges a fork into his salmon, takes a bite, and grins at me as he chews.

After a few minutes of eating, I give Oscar a perplexed stare as I swallow a bite of my lunch. "Oscar, if I tell you that my ideal Yellow Page client is anyone—"

"No!" Oscar reprimands, again slamming his hand down on the table, nearly startling me out of my seat. "Never use the words *anyone, someone,* or *everyone* in your description. You must be specific!"

I let out a sigh and regroup my thoughts. "Okay, if I tell you that my ideal Yellow Page client is a plumbing company based in the Portland-Vancouver metro area with thirty trucks, fifty employees, has a large advertising budget, loves getting emergency calls, needs to expand their business, and isn't currently working with another Yellow Page USA rep, would that be specific enough? 'Cause that's about as close to an ideal client as I could get."

"My boy," Oscar says through a mouth full of food with his arms spread open, a fork in one hand, and huge grin on his face. "I think you've got it!"

"But Oscar, I don't want to work with just plumbers. I've just eliminated every personal injury attorney who has a large advertising budget, is looking to expand their business, and isn't currently working with another Yellow Page USA rep. And I don't want to eliminate arborists or chiropractors. Those could be ideal clients too."

"Don't get your undies in a bunch, boy. You haven't eliminated anyone. Think of all of your possible ideal clients as the ingredients in a salad. I'm not asking you to describe a salad recipe. I just want a specific description of one ingredient," Oscar says, pointing around my plate with his fork. "Could be that arugula, could be that walnut, could be whatever that thing is there, could be a crouton. This part of the formula for hanging out requires a specific, detailed description of just one ideal client. And for the sake of this exercise your description of the plumber will do quite nicely. Now eat before you waste away." He gestures for me to continue eating and returns his full attention to his lunch.

The lull in our conversation allows me to become acutely aware of our surroundings. I eavesdrop on the lunchtime conversations around us, complimented by the cacophony of clanking dishes, a distant tugboat whistle, and the accordion now playing a slow version of "O' Sole Mio." The muggy mid-day air reminds me of a meal I ate in the French Quarter during a childhood trip to New Orleans.

With the final bite of lunch, I set my fork on the empty lunch plate, and watch as Oscar wipes his hands with a napkin. "Tell you what. Let's order some dessert, then we'll talk about step number two," he says, bringing me out of my flashback. He looks toward the restaurant window and snaps his fingers. Sid arrives at our table immediately.

"You guys ready for the check?"

"What's on the dessert menu, Sid?" Oscar asks.

"Well, you've already had the gelato, Oscar. We also have a handmade spumoni, the best tiramisu on the planet, and egg creams in four flavors: chocolate, coffee, strawberry, and vanilla."

"You sold me on the tiramisu, and I'll have a cup of coffee with that, black."

"You got it, Oscar. What about you, Tyler?"

"Can I just get a double espresso, Sid?"

"Coming right up," Sid answers as he collects the dishes from the table.

Oscar continues our lesson over the rattling of plates and silverware. "For the sake of argument, let's call your client, in this case the plumber, the golden egg."

"All right."

~The Goose That Lays the Golden Egg~

"If I were to give you a choice of either a golden egg or a goose that lays golden eggs, which would you choose?"

"The goose, of course."

"Why?"

"If golden eggs are what I want, then a goose that just lays them would save me the trouble of trying to find them."

Oscar tells me my answer is on the money by tapping his nose with his forefinger. "To continue the metaphor, the goose that lays the golden egg is a referral source. That is step two of our target market brainstorming process. Figuring out whom, by nature of their business, has a network of your ideal clients. You described a plumbing contractor based in the Portland area with thirty trucks, fifty employees, a large advertising budget, who loves getting emergency calls, needs to expand their business and isn't currently working with another Yellow Page rep as an ideal client. That is the egg. Who has a network of such creatures? Who's the goose?"

I shrug my shoulders. "General contractors, I guess."

"Let's explore this. General contractors would surely know plumbing contractors. But would they have a network of them?"

"Hmm . . . maybe, then again, maybe not. They'd all have at least one or two they sub-contracted work out to, but for most, that would probably be all. Okay, how about a plumbing supply outfit?"

"They, by nature of their business, would have to have a network of plumbers," Oscar says. "That could be a goose. Write that down. Who else would have a network of plumbing contractors?"

"Gosh, Oscar, I'm not a plumber. I don't really know."

"How about business coaches and associations?"

"There must be a plumbing contractor's association, but I don't get how a business coach would have a network of plumbing contractors."

"It would be a specific kind of coach. A plumber's consultant or business coach."

"Do plumbing contractors have business coaches?"

"The smart ones do."

"So how do I find them?"

"My boy, you live in an incredibly magical age. I suggest you take advantage of it. You have with you a device that has the capability of gathering the information you seek effortlessly. Yesterday you told me you could locate any business, and find out any information you needed about them, using that gizmo of yours. Can you give me a demonstration?"

"Sure! What am I looking for?"

"The business examples we just spoke of. Let's start with plumbing supply companies located in the greater Portland area."

I type *Portland wholesale plumbing supplies* into the search field on my phone and discover several plumbing supply outfits. "Wow, there's a bunch of them! Okay, let's see what I find if I type in *plumbing contractors business coach.*" In an instant, a company with a website that says *Business Training and Coaching for Plumbing Contractors* pops up. "Oscar, this is amazing. I never would have guessed there'd be a business coach for plumbers."

"Now type in *plumbing contractor's association*. I assure you it exists," he says smugly while fogging his glasses and then rubbing them with his handkerchief.

I type in *Oregon plumbing contractor's association*, and the search engine returns *Association of Plumbing, Heating and Cooling Contractors*. My heart begins to race. Still unclear about how to use this information, the possibilities begin to enter my mind from all sides. "I think I'm beginning to understand. I've been focusing my energy on finding people who'll buy ads. It makes more sense to build relationships with people who, by nature of their business, have a network of the people who need Yellow Page ads."

"Tell me why."

"Well, it's going to be a lot easier to find my plumbers who want to advertise in the directory by meeting them through the Plumbing Contractor's Association or through wholesale plumbing supply companies than it would be by pounding on doors, for one."

"Now you're gettin' the idea. Tell me, how would this apply to your financial services venture?"

"Of course!" I respond enthusiastically, the realization that the whole point of our lessons is to get my distributorship with Slarrefer Mutual up and running. "I need to make up some ideal clients who need what Slarrefer offers. But once I've identified them, I don't go looking for them, I seek out those who have networks of them. And since there's a business opportunity side of Slarrefer, people who have networks of people who are ideal clients for Slarrefer would be more likely to want to become a distributor, since it fits in with what they're already up to. Oscar, it's like I've been driving a car without knowing there was an accelerator, and you just showed me where the gas pedal is!" I yell, nearly jumping out of my seat.

"Calm down before you wet your pants. You're just beginning to see the potential. There's still another piece to it, a quantum leap in the thinking process, if you will. Let's talk about the granny goose."

~The Granny Goose~

"The granny goose?"

"Yes, the granny goose. Your target market is that person or entity that has a network of people who have a network of people who would use your product or service. If your client is the egg, and the person or entity that has a network of your client is the goose that lays the golden egg, then the—"

I can't stop myself from interrupting. "Then the person who has the network of people who have a network of my ideal client would be the granny goose!"

"You catch on fast, boy. *That* is your target market. And to think, a few minutes ago you were tripping over your own tongue to try to say that."

Sid returns and places Oscar's dessert and my espresso on the table. "Pretty lively conversation you guys got going on over here."

"This guy's rocking my world, Sid!" I exclaim, pointing both my index fingers at Oscar.

"The kid's been living under a rock, Sid. I'm just showing him the light of day," he says while again smugly rubbing his fingernails on his shirt and then looking at them.

"Glad to hear you're enjoying yourselves," he says as he places the check in the middle of the table. "You fellas have a good day."

"Thanks, Sid," we reply in unison.

I take a sip of my espresso and let out a sigh as I watch Oscar relish a bite of his tiramisu with his eyes closed. "I'm going to have to get back to the office soon, Oscar. This afternoon is the Tuesday phone-a-thon."

"What the hell is a foneython?"

"A phone-a-thon is when all the sales reps sit in the office for three straight hours calling businesses to set appointments for Yellow Page presentations. Our managers make a contest out of it. Whoever books the most appointments gets a spiff, like a dinner for two at Jake's or tickets to a Trailblazers game or something like that. None of the reps like doing it, though, because people become very upset when we interrupt them at their place of business. They just hang up on us. But thanks to you, my friend, today is going to be different for me," I say, holding up the stack of cards I collected this morning.

"Well, you go do whatever you need to do," he says, wiping his mouth after polishing off his desert in just three bites. "When we meet up for our next lesson, you can tell me how it went."

"What's our next lesson?"

"Networking 101: how to locate your geese and granny geese and strategically build relationships with them. In the meantime, I have a homework assignment for you. I want you to follow the formula for identifying your target market and come up with two examples of granny geese for the business you really want to be working at, that Slimyfer Mutual thing."

"It's Slarrefer!"

"Whatever. Be prepared to describe for me two ideal clients, their corresponding referral sources, and the target market for each."

I confirm his instructions by holding up one finger at a time. "You want me to, one, identify two ideal clients, and two, identify who, by nature of their business, has a network of those clients, and three, identify who, by nature of their business, has a network of the networks of people who would be my ideal client?"

Oscar claps his hands. "Very impressive. Even I might have twisted my tongue on that one."

I can't help the grin taking over my face. Oscar's approval makes me feel like a ten year old who just hit the game winning home run in front of his father. As I stand to leave, I realize my time today with him has come to an end. I resist a strong compulsion to give him a hug. "Oscar, thanks for your help. I don't know how or why you're here, but it sure means a lot to me."

"Don't mention it, kid. I'm getting as much out of this as you are," he replies as he stares at the lunch check, piquing my curiosity. Does my teapot-dwelling confidante use cash or credit cards? He removes his glasses, places them in his shirt pocket, pushes his chair back, and stands up to leave.

"What do you say we pick this up tomorrow? Where you gonna be?"

"I have to canvas a few blocks just west of here, between Eighteenth and Twenty-Third. The businesses are kind of spread out there, so I'll be doing more walking than talking. I should be done by two o'clock at the latest," I answer as my attention is drawn to the sky by a sudden gray pall falling over the neighborhood. I watch the bright sun disappear behind a dark cloud. "An afternoon storm to cool things off would sure feel nice," I exclaim, turning to look back at Oscar.

He's gone. Before me now stands a severe looking middle-aged woman wearing a dirty apron, chewing a piece of gum, holding an order pad and pencil.

"Can I get you something?" she says in a gravelly voice, obviously rough from decades of cigarette smoke. The sour expression on her face gives me the impression she just bit down on a bee.

"Where's Oscar?"

"Who?"

"My friend, Oscar. He was just standing right there, where you are, not one second ago. Mid-sixties, dark hair, goatee, looks like cross between a bulldog and a tank."

"I don't know any Oscar. What're you having to eat?"

"Nothing thanks. I'm stuffed. Sid took care of us."

"Who?"

"Sid, the guy who waited on us."

"There's no one here named Sid," she replies with a harsh tone. "Look, these tables are for customers only."

"But I just ate lunch here. I had the arugula salad."

"We don't have no arugula salad," she scowls. "Coffee and sandwiches. That's it. So if you're not going to buy anything, take a hike."

"He did it to me again," I mutter under my breath with embarrassment as I turn to start back to the car.

"I get all the weirdos," she grumbles as she turns away.

The walk to the car gives me just enough time to make myself nuts trying to process what happened over the last several hours. *Does he exist or doesn't he? I'm still full from the lunch he bought me, the lunch the waitress claimed they didn't serve. I did walk my route. That's where I'm walking back from . . . Wait! My route! The cards I gathered from the businesses I visited!* I reach into my pocket. To my relief they're there. *So I did really walk my route.* I look at the notes I made on the back of the cards as I walk. *Okay, so those conversations did happen. Then why is it that after I meet with Oscar it's like the conversation never took place and he never existed? The time! What time is it?*

I look at my phone: 1:30. *So I did just spend two hours . . . someplace. I remember the lunch. I remember the conversation and Sid the waiter, and especially the colorful stories Oscar told me to make his point about identifying an ideal client.*

My internal dialogue bubbles up into unconscious muttering. "He's got to be real. Please may he be real. He's like the best friend I ever had . . . or never had. Oh man, I'm losing it." As I continue to mumble, the sound of approaching footsteps prompts me to look up from the sidewalk. A boy holding a skateboard headed in the opposite direction shoots me a judgmental look accentuated by a raised eyebrow.

The southern sky continues to darken as I draw closer to the car. I'm so distracted by my own thoughts I hardly notice the flickering in the dark sky above the West Hills and the Portland skyline. Thunder rumbles in the distance as I put the key in the car door.

"I've got to focus. *I did* meet all these people today. *I do* have their cards, *and they do* want to get together to find out how we might network with each other. This morning *did* happen," I try hard to convince myself. "He is real. He disappeared on me yesterday, but was right back where he said he would be today. Before he disappeared today, he said he would meet me in the field tomorrow. So what am I getting all worked up about?"

I close the car door and start the engine. Before putting the car into gear, I see the teapot on the passenger side floor. I reach down to pick it up. The feeling of electricity tingles in my hands and surges through my body as I put the teapot in my lap. It's not an uncomfortable feeling. But it is weird, a little like the feeling you get when you touch your tongue to the business end of a new nine-volt battery. I remove the lid and peek inside. Nothing. I place the teapot back on the floor, force my mind to quiet the riot of thoughts it's been trying to process, and stare straight ahead over the steering wheel. A giant raindrop plops on my windshield as I put the car in gear and head for the office.

The Golden Egg

An ideal client that I make up. The person
or entity that puts money in my pocket.
(Specific description)

My ideal Yellow Page client
Plumbing contractor
- Based in Portland/Vancouver area
- 30+ trucks
- 50+ employees
- Large advertising budget
- Loves getting emergency calls
- Needs to expand
- Not working with another Yellow Page rep

The Goose that lays the Golden Egg
A person or entity who, by nature of their
business, would have a network of people
who need my service.
- Plumbing supply shops?
- Business coach?
- Plumbers association

The Granny Goose
The person or entity who, by nature of
their business, would have a network of
people who have a network of people who
need my service.

Seven

Pillow Talk

Rain taps at the bedroom window accompanied by a tree branch scraping against the outside of our apartment wall. After a long and teary conversation earlier this evening, Karen and I made up. I've been allowed back into the bedroom, but my sleep is interrupted by anxiety about our finances and my job. It's too hot to sleep, anyway. Though the storm is cooling things off outside, the apartment still feels like an oven. I squirm, sticky from perspiration. The additional worrying about how hard it's going to be to function tomorrow, exhausted from yet another poor night's sleep, makes me even more restless. I wonder what time it is. Without looking at the clock, I guess that it's two o'clock. Seems like it's always two o'clock when I wake in the middle of the night.

Yesterday's events flood my mind. All those business cards I collected, the ideas Oscar shared with me. I can't stop wondering if he's real or just a symptom of yet another problem: that I'm losing my mind from stress. I can't argue with the results I achieved during the past afternoon's office phone-a-thon by following his advice. It was a completely different experience this time. No one hung up on me. I was greeted with friendly voices appreciative that I was getting back to them so soon. Everyone was eager to set a time to have me swing by so we could learn about each other's business. Instead of being the struggling new guy, I was the one who set the most appointments in the office.

I rest my arm on my forehead and let my eyes play tricks in the dark as I stare straight up from the bed at the ceiling. Pinpricks of light dance in the darkness whether my eyes are open or closed.

"Hey, you okay?" Karen whispers, as she turns over and rubs my chest, interrupting a cacophony of thoughts.

"I thought you were asleep," I answer.

"How can I sleep with the sound of you worrying?"

"The sound of me worrying?"

"Yes, your loud sighs and twitching are the sounds of you worrying."

"What makes you think I wasn't sleeping?"

"Freight train snoring is the sound of you sleeping. What's on your mind?"

I've never been able to lie to Karen, she knows me too well. But I don't dare tell her about Oscar. She'll think I've lost it for sure. I try to avoid the subject by becoming defensive. "When we first got married, you used to complain about my snoring. Now you're telling me you can't sleep because I'm not snoring?"

I don't get an answer, just a moment of silence followed by the click and harsh light of the nightstand lamp. "So what's on your mind?"

Okay, getting defensive didn't work. She's got me. I have to tell her something. I give it my best shot without giving her too much information. I turn over and lean my head on my elbow and look into her dark brown eyes. The first time I saw her, those eyes were the first thing I was attracted to. They have an irresistible effect on me, one that makes it impossible to lie to her.

"I met someone the other day, a very successful businessman. He's offered to help me build my Slarrefer business. I was just thinking about what he and I talked about."

"Where'd you meet him?"

"At the Tea Zone."

"Tell me about him."

Damn! How does she do it? I'm just lying here, safe inside my own head, and in thirty-seconds she's kicking down the door of my deepest, darkest secret.

"I was having a tea in the lounge, and we just ended up sharing a table. He's sort of a New Yorker, but he built a very successful manufacturing business in the Middle East. He's retired now and spends his time mentoring people like me."

"How did you end up sharing a table with him?"

That's it, I'm stuffed. If I tell her the truth, she'll think I've lost it and leave me for good. Or she'll have me committed, or both. But if I lie, she'll know it. I put my arm around her neck, lay back down, bring her head to my chest and hold her tight. Her jet-black hair smells like a sweet tropical forest.

"Okay, I'll tell you if you promise not to get upset or tell me I need to see a shrink."

"Sweetheart, your chest is pounding. Please tell me you didn't give this guy any money."

"You have to promise."

"I already think you need to see a shrink," she says jokingly. I don't respond, too distraught to see the humor.

"Okay, okay, I promise I won't get upset."

A moment passes while I gather my thoughts. "No, I haven't given him a cent. In fact, he spent money on me. He bought me a delicious lunch today. He's one of the neatest people I've ever met, a real character. He talks a little like an east coast construction worker, but he's full of really practical business wisdom that's easy to understand. He's fun and easy to be with. He's kind of like the dad I wish I could have had growing up, but he's also an amazing friend who's taken me under his wing."

"How long have you known this guy?"

"Umm, a couple of days."

"In a couple of days this guy's become an amazing friend, and is like a dad to you? Tyler, what have you done?"

"I haven't done anything."

"Then why were you afraid to tell me about him?"

"Cause you'll think I've gone crazy if I tell you the truth. I'm not even sure I haven't gone crazy."

She lifts her head from my chest, rolls over on her elbow, and props her head up with her hand. "All right," she says with a long sigh. "Neither one of us is going to get any sleep now, so why don't you just tell it to me from the beginning."

Here it comes. Resigned to heading for the couch after this conversation, I reach over to the glass on the night stand, take a drink of water, lay back with a loud exhale, and tell Karen the whole story, starting with the migraine that hit me Monday afternoon. I recount the experience of the teapot, Oscar, and what he's been teaching me. I finish by telling her about my homework assignment for tonight, coming up with two geese and two granny geese. I lay silently for what seems an eternity waiting for a reaction. I get nothing.

"Go ahead, say it. You think I've lost my mind."

"Sweetie, I can tell you believe everything you just told me, and it scares me. I think you're stressed out beyond the point of being healthy. Of course, I'm not going to believe for a second this guy is 2,500 years old and lives in a teapot. But everything you say he's taught you actually seems to make really good sense."

"Want me to go sleep on the couch?"

"No, you better stay right here."

"Are you going to have me committed?"

"We can't afford that." We both burst out laughing. "Tell you what," she struggles to say through worried giggles, "As long as you're getting good advice from this guy, I'll look the other way about the other stuff. But if he starts telling you to spend money in weird places, tells you to jump off a bridge, hurt yourself or anyone else, then you need to tell me so we can get you some help."

"It's a deal."

"Am I going to get to meet this character?" she asks.

"I don't know. Like I told you, one minute he's there, the next he's gone. I s'pose I can ask him," I answer, feeling myself begin to nod off.

"I love you baby, but I'm really worried about you," she says, rubbing my forehead.

"I love you too. I'll be okay as long as I've got you." I squeeze her hard and give her a kiss filled with appreciation for how lucky I am to have her. With my burden lifted, I promptly drift into a deep sleep.

EIGHT

Did You Do Your Homework?

It's just after one on Wednesday afternoon, and I'm unlocking the car after returning from canvasing the Northwest District neighborhood between NW Twenty-Third and Eighteenth. Last night's rain broke the heat spell. Now the streets have dried, and the temperature has risen to a relatively comfortable high-seventies. After only a partial night's sleep, I had some trouble getting started this morning, so I thought a stroll might help clear out the cobwebs. I strategically parked the Saturn at the intersection of NW Eighteenth and Glisan, at the last address on today's route, walked up to NW Twenty-Third, and then worked my way back to the car. It worked. I'm invigorated by the rain-washed air saturated with the smell of damp ground and wet rotting wood from the century-old trees that grow alongside the streets. I take a seat in the Saturn and sift through the business cards I'd collected while I chow down yesterday's uneaten lunch that I'd kept chilled overnight.

After chewing the last section of tangerine, I check the time on my phone: 1:32 p.m. I scroll over to the calendar and see the appointment to hang out tomorrow morning with Nadia and Anton, the owners of the medical supply store, and another two-dozen or so appointments over the next couple of weeks. "I'm going to have to start pacing myself," I say aloud. Although the advice Oscar's given me makes perfect sense, the fact remains that I've only got three-and-a-half weeks to hit my sales quota. Familiar pangs of doubt dance with my lunch deep in my stomach. I'm beginning to understand the long-term possibilities of Oscar's strategy, but that doesn't change the fact that I'm likely to be unemployed by the end of the coming month.

I look down at the teapot sitting on the passenger side floor and pick it up for reassurance. The ornate metal feels cool to the touch, but that's it, no tingly feeling. "Guess you're not home," I say aloud. I set the teapot back down and stare out the window at the heavily tree-shaded neighborhood. Thoughts of concern, bordering on panic, rattle around my brain as my eyes unconsciously settle on the front window of a coffee house and pastry shop just across the intersection. The glass of the window reflects the sunlit side of the street, where the car is parked. I focus on the reflection, mesmerized by a visual game that starts up in my head: me watching myself sitting across the street in the car across the street from me. Adjusting my eyesight to see through the reflection into the shop, I squint to see if I can make anything out. A round figure waving through the glass suddenly registers.

"Oscar!" I blurt out, relieved and excited to see him.

I quickly gather up my briefcase, scramble out of the car, lock the door, and make my way across the street. Upon entering the eatery, I walk past the register and around to the left where Oscar sits, crumbs and powdered sugar surrounding his overstuffed mouth. An expression of delight—no, make that ecstasy—beams from his face as he chews. As I take in the endearing sight, he motions for me to sit down.

"Well you're certainly a vision. How'd you get here?" I ask with surprise.

His mouth too full to speak, Oscar spreads his arms and rocks back and forth, mimicking flight. I decide it would be better not to inquire any further. He pushes a plate of round, powdered-sugar-coated pastries across the table to me, points at an item on the menu laying on the lacquer-coated wooden table, and takes another bite while rubbing his belly, his non-verbal way of telling me it's delicious. I look to where he's pointing. It reads *Sesame Fried Crushed Almond-Cardamom Balls*. He licks his fingers, then brings his thumb, middle finger, and forefinger to his lips, and kisses them away as he again rubs his large stomach in a wide circular motion with his other hand. His euphoria is contagious. My spirit soars at watching my mentor eat. "I don't think I've ever seen anyone enjoy eating as much you!" I laugh.

Like an old-world Italian mama encouraging her boy to eat up, he vigorously motions for me to join him. Three pastries remain on the plate. I pick one up and take a bite. The delicate texture and blend of exotic flavors is both very unusual and delicious.

"Reminds me a little of a dish back home called *al-salooq*," he mumbles through a mouth still partially full as he reaches across the table for another pastry. "So how'd your phoney-thing go yesterday?" he asks, examining the cardamom ball he's just picked up.

"You mean the phone-a-thon? I called back all the people I met on my route yesterday that told me they were open to meeting with me. I set the most appointments of anyone in the office!" I declare proudly.

"That's a big improvement over getting thrown out of every door you walk through," he replies as he plops the cardamom ball in his mouth.

"I'll say. In fact, six more people from this morning's route want to get together too. It's amazing how a minor tweak in my approach can have such a huge effect on my results."

He closes his eyes and chews thoughtfully. After a moment, he opens his eyes and lets out a satisfied sigh. "The only result you've achieved was to schedule appointments," he replies stoically. "Remember, the goal is to get you hanging out for a living, not setting appointments for a living. We still have a lot of work to do on you," he barks while wiping his face with a napkin. "So whaddya say we get to today's lesson?"

"I'm ready!" I anxiously answer, pointing out a spot of powdered sugar on his cheek that he missed.

"Did you do your homework?"

"Yup," I answer as I pull out my notepad.

"Tell me what you came up with for target markets for your Swarmy business?"

"It's Slarrefer," I correct. I'm not sure if I'm more amused or agitated by Oscar's seemingly deliberate mispronunciations.

"Yeah, that's what I said. So whatcha got? Give it to me from the beginning. Who's your ideal client?"

~Target Market Number One~

"Okay, my first ideal client would be a couple between the ages of thirty and fifty who're in good health, have a combined income of at least one hundred thousand dollars per year, have children, live in the greater Portland/Vancouver metro area, and are financially vulnerable."

Oscar writes *Couple w/kids—underinsured—100k* on the notepad and then stares at it for a moment.

"Explain to me what you mean by financially vulnerable?"

"They're either uninsured or underinsured. If anything happens to one of them, be it a health issue, an accident, or death, they could lose everything because they don't have life insurance, long-term disability insurance, or long-term care insurance."

"Is that a description of a client you're attracted to? Your ideal client should be someone who you get satisfaction in serving above and beyond the monetary reward. Is this a client you'd love to work with?"

"Yeah, it is. My grandparents fit that description when they were alive, but they didn't have the kind of help Slarrefer provides. I don't ever want anyone to die alone in a strange nursing home like my grandfather did. He spent the last years of his life regretting that he didn't have the resources to get my grandmother the kind of medical care that would have kept her from dying before he did. I just feel called to help people like that.

"I gotta tell you, Oscar, this exercise really opened me up to why I'm doing this. It's the piece that's been missing from everything else I've ever tried. In the past, I'd pursue an opportunity not because it fulfilled me, but because I thought it was a way to pay my bills, or because there was some promise that I could get rich. With Slarrefer, I feel I can make a real difference. That gets me excited."

"And that, my boy, is an indication that you're on the right path. Good work. This sounds like a well-defined golden egg. So whom did you come up with as the goose that would be the source of such eggs?"

"Portland based CPAs, bookkeepers, and tax specialists. They, by nature of their business, would likely have such clients."

Oscar nods his head while stroking his chin with his familiar raised eyebrow of approval, again letting me know he's impressed at my answer. "Very good. So who could be the granny goose?"

"The granny goose could be a manager of some kind for a Portland-based payroll services company."

"How did you arrive at that?" he asks with a puzzled tone.

"Payroll service companies have networks of CPAs, tax specialists, and bookkeepers."

"Enlighten me. How would payroll service companies have networks of CPAs, tax specialists, and bookkeepers?"

"Well, I was talking to one of Slarrefer's top reps last night. He told me that the reason he's so successful is because he used to work for one of the big payroll companies in town. Apparently, it's common practice in the industry for an accountant to refer clients to a payroll company when the client's payroll needs outgrow the accountant's ability to effectively handle the work load."

"So he already had a network of geese?"

"Yeah. He told me that when he joined Slarrefer he got in touch with his network of accountants and all of them had clients who would be good candidates for Slarrefer's financial package. But it seemed to me that tax specialists and bookkeepers would also have business relationships like that."

Oscar finishes drawing out the three-step target market genealogy while still nodding his head with approval. "Nice work, kid! I can tell you're going to make me proud."

Target market #1

(Golden egg)　Couple w/kids
100k
under-insured

↓

(Goose)　Accountants/Bookkeepers
Tax specialists

↓

(Granny goose)　Payroll service companies　　Target market

Target market #2

Couple between fifty and seventy
In Portland/Vancouver area
Grown children
Are financially well off
Retired or close to it
Legacy for heirs

(Golden egg)

(Goose)

Estate Planning Attorneys

Target market

(Granny goose)

Bar Association?

~Target Market Number Two~

He flips the top sheet of my notepad to the blank page underneath. "So tell me who your second target market is. This time, start with who the target is, and then explain to me how you identified them."

"Okay. My second target is the bar association."

"And how did you arrive at that?"

"Well, the golden egg is an individual or a couple between the ages of fifty and seventy who live in the greater Portland/Vancouver metropolitan area, have grown children, are financially well off, are retired or close to retirement, and are looking for a way to preserve a financial legacy for their heirs."

"And who are their heirs?"

"Usually it's their children and grandchildren. But it could also be another relative, a non-profit or some kind of charity, a spouse or a domestic partner—pretty much anyone they want it to be."

Oscar nods his head with approval. "Again, another well-defined golden egg. So who's the goose?"

"I came up with a few, but estate planning attorneys topped the list."

Oscar scribbles on the fresh sheet from my pad and exclaims, "Yes, yes! Very good! And you determined that the bar association would, by nature of who it serves, have a network of estate planning attorneys?"

"Yup," I reply smugly.

Oscar claps loudly and roars "Beautiful!" He then collapses into an expressionless stare. "So how would a man with no legal background, and next to no working experience in his chosen field, penetrate the bar association? And who would he expect to hang out with there?"

"I have no idea, Oscar. I was hoping you could help me with that. I did do some googling last night. Turns out there's the National Bar Association, the Oregon State Bar Association, about as many county bars as there are counties, as well as a couple of neighborhood bar associations in the Portland area. But that's as far as I got."

He writes *Bar Association?* then taps the notepad with the eraser end of his pencil as he continues.

"Hmm . . . in that case, the bar association is only a potential granny goose, but you did follow the formula, and I'll give credit for that. You simply need to gather more information. However, you're on the right track. In this lesson, we're going to stick with how to determine who the right people to network with are. We'll cover where to find them later. At that time, I'll show you how to go about networking within associations and other business organizations."

"Good, 'cause I wouldn't have a clue where to begin."

"Not to worry. It's simple stuff. So you have two target markets: payroll company sales representatives and the bar association. Let's add some clarity to the rather vague description of your target markets. Try adding a *whom* to your description."

"A *whom*?"

"Yes, a specific person. Let's say you're hanging out over coffee with someone you met at a networking event, and the topic of conversation comes around to whom you want to be introduced to. Telling them that a good referral for you would be an introduction to a sales manager for a local payroll company isn't going to be as effective as asking for an introduction to Bob Smith, the sales manager at Acme Payroll."

"You mean give them the actual name of someone who fits the description of my target market?"

"That's right."

"So I need to find the name of a person at the bar association as well."

"Exactly. Again, we'll get into how to figure out whom to meet at an industry association a little later. In any case, you'll be amazed at how many people will already have a personal relationship with those you want to be introduced to, especially in a close-knit city like Portland. But it'll be a lot easier for people to introduce you to whom you want to meet if you give them the name of a person rather than just a job title."

~*Why Do I Need an Introduction?*~

"But if I already know the name of someone who fits the profile of my granny goose, why would I need an introduction? Can't I just look them up online and connect with them that way?"

The expression on Oscar's face collapses into a blank, frustrated stare. "Of course you could," he says, rolling his eyes. "And how would you go about doing that?"

"Well, most business people are on LinkedIn. I can send a connection request."

"And why would this person accept you as a connection?"

"Most people accept connections, Oscar. The more connections you have, the better you look."

"According to whom?"

"Well, it's just common practice. It's impressive if you have lots of connections."

Oscar raises his signature eyebrow of disapproval. "Tell you what. We'll have a conversation about networking through social media in another lesson. Let's stick with this discussion. Assuming he or she accepts you as a connection, now what?"

"Just call them up, I s'pose," I reply meekly, aware that I've said something that's frustrated Oscar.

"Okay, let's say I'm Joe Smith over at Acme Payroll, and let's say you actually got me on the phone directly. You've told me your name, and I ask what I can do for you.

Your turn," Oscar says with arms folded and a look that dares me to get out of the dead end I've just talked myself into.

"Umm . . . Joe, I was wondering if I could buy you a cup of coffee and talk about referring business to each other."

"And what is your business?" Oscar coldly replies.

"I'm with Slarrefer Mutual, a financial services and insurance company."

"Never heard of 'em. And what kind of business were you thinking of referring to us?"

"Well, uh, that's what I wanted to talk to you about."

"I'm quite busy. Why do we have to have coffee? What is it we can't talk about over the phone?"

"Well I, uh . . . "

Oscar mercifully ends the exercise with the gentleness of a drill sergeant. "You can quit yer stammerin'. I think you get the point."

"Okay, now I understand. I'm explaining that a great referral for me would be an *introduction*," I say emphatically, "to Bob Smith so I don't have to call him cold."

"That's the whole point, isn't it?" Oscar asks. "If you cold-call Bob for the purpose of hanging out he will likely resist. Put yourself in his shoes. A stranger calls out of the blue and wants to get together for coffee to discuss referring business. What would be your response?"

"Depends on what that person says, I suppose. I can see myself accepting the offer depending upon the feeling I got from the call. But I admit I'd also be suspicious of what that person's true agenda was."

"Fair enough. Now let's say a friend or trusted business acquaintance called and said he had someone you had to meet."

"I'd say sure!"

"Even though you had no idea who the person was?"

I ponder the question for a moment. "I'd of course ask who, why and where, but the decision to take the meeting would be based solely on the fact that my friend said I should meet this person and that he'd facilitate the introduction."

"And there you have the answer to the question *If you know who you want to meet, why do you need an introduction rather than call them directly?* When you're introduced to someone who may be a possible golden egg, goose, or granny goose, the relationship starts from a very different place than it does if you were to cold-call that same person for the purpose of starting a relationship."

I stare at the notepad, pausing to reflect upon our conversation. After a few moments, my present financial situation and the fact that I'm now twenty-seven days away from being fired if I don't bring $55,000 in revenue begins to erode at the wisdom that's been shared with me. I look up at the burly vision sitting across the table. Somehow he knows what I'm about to ask, and somehow I know he knows, but I ask anyway.

"Oscar, there's a voice in my head that sounds like my manager arguing with this process. The voice says that in the amount of time it would take for me to hang out with people, educate them on the kind of referrals I'm looking for, get them to talk to my target market, and then arrange an introduction, I could have made like a zillion cold calls. Even if I only got one appointment a day, it would be faster than how long all this is going to take."

"Didn't we just have this conversation the other day? Granted, it is going to take some time to grow the garden. But I can tell you from personal experience, the harvest is well worth the time and effort. Besides, if it was in your nature to make a zillion cold calls, then you wouldn't need my help, and we wouldn't be having this conversation."

"Touché," I reply with a resigned sigh, still torn between the excitement I feel for applying what Oscar's teaching me and the worry that, at this point, nothing short of a miracle will keep me from getting fired from my job.

We both stare at the last remaining cardamom ball. Oscar picks it up, breaks it in two, and offers me half. "Any more questions about whom you should spend your time building business relationships with?"

"No, it's actually pretty simple. Just takes a different way of thinking to grasp the concept. But I have a lot of questions about actually hanging out with people. I have an appointment to meet with the folks at that medical supply store tomorrow morning. It's my first hang out, and I don't want to screw it up."

"Of course you do. You'll never master anything without screwing it up first. Those who don't make mistakes never accomplish anything."

"I get your meaning. Let me put it another way. I'd like to get the best result possible from my first hang out."

"Now *that* I can help you with. Assuming that you can get through this first meeting without burning these people's business down, then any mistake short of that will simply be a valuable learning experience."

"Now that would be a mistake!"

"Yes it would. However, I have complete faith that you can get through your meeting and leave these people's business intact," Oscar says. "But since you brought it up, I suggest we continue our discussion so we can cover how to have a productive hang out."

I look at the time: 2:45. I had planned on being home by three to make my follow-up calls. "I've got to go make some calls, but I should be done by about four thirty. Can we get back together then?"

"Certainly," Oscar replies. A sinister expression suddenly comes across his face as he looks around the room. "It's my understanding that you enjoy a good cigar," he says quietly, like he's suggesting we do something illegal.

"Yeah, but I haven't been able to afford them lately. How'd you know I like cigars?"

"I have my ways."

"So, you smoke cigars?" I ask, delighted at the prospect of having a smoke with my ancient friend and curious as to how it is that he came to indulge, knowing that there were no such things as cigars in ancient Babylon.

"Oh, I've discovered many earthly delights in my journeys through the millennia," he says, waggling his eyebrows at me.

"In that case, let's meet someplace later for a cigar!"

"That was going to be my suggestion. You got a spot in mind?"

"There's a cool cigar lounge not too far from our apartment in Lake Oswego called Broadway Cigars."

"I'll find it."

I open my phone calendar and add the appointment for four thirty. "It's on the calendar," I say as I look up from the phone at the now empty seat across the table from me. The booth is spotless, as if it had just been bussed. No sign of Oscar or the cardamom balls. Not even a crumb. I quickly gather my belongings and leave before being faced with another awkward encounter with a server.

NINE

Hanging Out

"How can I help you?" a man in his early sixties asks cheerfully as I enter the Broadway Cigar shop in Lake Oswego, an affluent suburb of Portland, about eight miles south of downtown Portland.

"I'm supposed to meet someone here for a cigar."

"Have you been here before?"

"Yeah, but it's been a while. Okay if we hang out in the back lounge?"

"Sure, as long as you buy a cigar. Whaddya smoke?"

"You carry Camachos?"

"We sure do," he replies, motioning for me to follow him into the walk-in humidor where the cigars are stored to maintain their moisture content.

The cigar shop houses two separate lounges, one in front and the other in back. The front lounge has eight artificial leather armchairs surrounding a coffee table in the middle of the room. The walls are painted deep maroon, decorated with framed black-and-white photos of famous cigar smokers from Winston Churchill and George Burns to Sigmund Freud and Groucho Marx.

"By the way, I'm Doug," he says as we enter the humidor.

I reach out to shake his hand. "I'm Tyler. Pleasure to meet you, Doug."

"Good to meet you too, Tyler. I've been expecting you. Your friend Oscar's already in the back."

"He is? You've seen him?"

He gives me a puzzled look. "No, I'm psychic," he replies sarcastically. "Whaddya mean have I seen him? He bought a cigar and told me he was expecting you. Besides, a character like that's kind of hard to miss." His response tells me he's obviously unaware of Oscar's otherworldly nature. I look around the humidor lined with stacks of cedar shelves displaying open boxes of cigars. Doug leads me to a corner with several varieties of the Camacho, retrieves one from a box, and hands me the large cigar for inspection. "Ever try the Giganté?"

"Can't say I have. Is this a natural or Connecticut?" I ask, referring to the outer leaf that wraps the cigar.

"Actually, that's a Corojo. It's a little bolder than a natural, but not too strong. It's become a favorite around here."

I look at the price, relatively inexpensive for a cigar that size, but more than I can afford given my limited resources. I turn my attention around the room to see if I can spot something within my budget. Seeing my reaction to the price, Doug gives me knowing look. "Your friend's got you covered. Get whatever you want."

I hold the cigar up with delight. "In that case, I'll give it a try!"

As soon as we step out of the humidor, the rich smell of cigar smoke from two gentleman watching a wide-screen plasma TV mounted on the wall instantly transports me back to my fifth birthday, when the aroma of my grandfather's after-dinner cigar, and the family singing "Happy Birthday," left a permanent memory.

"You want me to cut that for you?" Doug asks.

"I can handle it. You got a punch?"

"Sure do," he replies, pointing out a cigar punch lying on the cluttered counter. "There's also a fresh brewed pot of coffee if you'd like a cup before you settle in." He offers me a light as I remove the plug from the end of the cigar. I take a draw, rotating it to get an even light, and let out a large cloud of smoke. He snaps the lighter closed and points to the doorway leading to the dimly lit back lounge. "Your friend's waiting for you in the back. If you need anything else, don't hesitate to ask."

"Thanks, Doug!" I pour myself a Styrofoam cup full of coffee and step into the back lounge, which looks a lot like the front, but much bigger. In the center of the lounge is a pool table. To the right are two faux leather couches facing each other with a coffee table in the middle. Behind them is a tall cabinet housing individual cigar lockers for regular customers. Around the lounge, several small tables, each illuminated by a reading lamp and armchairs on either side, line the walls. And there seated comfortably in the corner to my left is Oscar, puffing on a very large cigar.

~Always Be Prepared to Make a Sale~

"Tylowitz!" he shouts upon seeing me enter the room. He motions for me to take a seat by patting the arm of the chair next him. "Whatcha smokin', kid?"

"Camacho Giganté," I answer. I place my coffee on the table between the chairs, perch my cigar in the notch of the large marble ashtray on the table between us, and settle into the opposite chair. "How 'bout 'bout you?"

"Jaime Garcia Reserva Especial," he answers, while examining it between his thumb and forefinger. "Smooth, creamy, a little woody with just a hint of pepper. Quite nice!" He takes another draw and closes his eyes to fully experience the flavor.

I take a draw from my cigar and gesture with it while releasing a thick cloud of smoke. "Thanks!"

"Don't mention it, kid. It's my pleasure," he answers while waving a dismissive hand. "A quiet lounge, fine cigar, and intelligent conversation with a good friend . . . " he pauses to take another puff and blows out the most perfect smoke ring I've ever seen, "Life doesn't get much better! So you ready to begin?"

I lay my notepad on my lap and remove the pen from my pocket. "Ready!"

"Write this down: always be prepared to make a sale."

"I finish writing, stare at Oscar, and then back at the sentence I just wrote, confounded by what seems like a sudden contradiction in everything Oscar's been teaching me.

"I thought you said that trying to sell people stuff is what's prevented me from being successful. Now you start this lesson by telling me to always be prepared to make a sale?"

"You got a problem with that?"

"Yeah. You've said repeatedly that in order to hang out for a living I should be building relationships, not trying to sell people stuff. Now you've just contradicted yourself."

"I've done no such thing," he responds with an annoying calmness.

With a frustrated sigh, I lay my pen on the notepad and wait for him to continue.

"There's a difference between trying to sell someone something they have not agreed to in advance and being prepared to make a sale in the event they are ready to buy. Being prepared to make a sale isn't the same as trying to make a sale. Let me put it another way. Always be prepared to provide the service for which you're paid."

"I'm still not following you."

"We've established that hanging out for a living is only possible if you do so in service to others, have we not?"

"Yeah."

"Therefore, it would be a great disservice if you were hanging out with someone and you discovered that they are in need of the service you provide and you were not prepared to fulfill that need."

"So you're saying that even though I'm not hanging out with someone with the intention of making a sale, I should be prepared to, just in case they want to buy?"

"Precisely."

"I think I understand what you're saying, but can you give it to me straight without being so cryptic?"

"It's your job to sell Yellow Page advertising, right?"

"Yeah."

"Before you make a sale, isn't there some preparation you must do?"

"It's a process, Oscar. First I contact people to set up an appointment to do a presentation. Once I've set the appointment, I have to prepare for the presentation."

"And what does such preparation entail?"

"Well, first I research their business to see what other advertising they're already doing and who their competition is. Then I mock up a demo ad so they can see what it might look like in our book."

"Then, before you hang out with anyone, I recommend that you make such preparations before you meet with them."

"But what if they're not a prospect? Why would I prepare to make a sale to someone who has no use for an ad?"

Oscar gives me a look like I just asked the dumbest question ever, draws on his cigar, replies, "You tell me," and closes his eyes.

Realizing he's in no hurry for my response, I take a puff of my cigar and take in the vision of the large man. Again it looks like he's gone into a deep meditation. In fact, as I look closely it doesn't appear that he's even breathing. As I ponder my response, I'm tempted to poke him to make sure he's still alive. After a moment of thought, the answer comes to me.

"Okay, the reason I always want to be prepared to sell an ad is because, even if they're not in the market, those I hang out with may have networks of people who may need advertising, and it's my job to educate them about how I can serve those people."

"And . . . ?" he says while slowly opening his eyes.

"Because it may turn out that they actually need an ad themselves?"

"Very good."

~Serving the Garden~

"Okay, but when are we going to get to the part about how I'm going to get people to refer business to me?"

Oscar gives me an intense but thoughtful stare. "Before we continue this lesson, we'd better clarify the attitude you must adopt before you begin hanging out with people. Write this down: you don't get others to introduce you to the people and networks you want to meet; you allow them to introduce you to those you want to meet. Just like you allowed the garden to give you cantaloupe. Therefore, the purpose of hanging out isn't to get others to do your bidding, but to get to know them well enough so that you may serve them by introducing them to the people and networks that will enrich their business."

"Hanging out in service to others!" I exclaim as I write.

He responds with an affirmative wink. "In time you'll discover that by strategically connecting people for their benefit they'll collectively do the same for you."

"Not sure what you mean by 'they'll collectively do the same for me.'"

"Put your notepad aside for a minute and enjoy your cigar. Let's just talk." He leans his head back and blows a cloud of smoke with a soft, satisfied puff. "The relational garden is made up of those in your network. Let's think of them as seeds, and the first time you hang out with someone, you're planting the seed. There's a critical distinction between serving the garden versus serving the seeds. Just as there were seeds in your cantaloupe garden that never produced fruit, despite the fact that you gave them the same care as the ones that did, there will also be individuals to whom you'll go to great lengths to bring value that will never reciprocate. In the relational garden, it is the activity of gardening that produces the harvest, not the rearing of seeds."

"Let me see if I'm getting the concept. I'm meeting with people to teach them how to identify their target markets. By doing so I'll get to know them and learn what kinds of people and networks would be beneficial for them to have me connect them to."

He nods.

I continue. "As I get to know more and more people, I'll inevitably meet those who would qualify as eggs, geese, and granny geese—not only for me, but for others. So as time goes on, my network of people grows, and as my network grows, the more valuable I become as a connector."

"Beautiful! Just beautiful!" Oscar exclaims, delighted at my understanding of the concept.

"So I'm serving the garden by nurturing each individual relationship, by sharing the hanging out formula with them, and through introductions to people and opportunities that I feel will benefit them. Some people will reciprocate and some won't. But you're saying that doesn't matter because the relational garden, as a whole, will provide the referrals and introductions that will grow my business?" I ask, understanding the concept, but still not completely convinced it can successfully work for me.

Oscar nods his head, frowning at his cigar because it has gone out. "The lessons learned from your early gardening endeavor will serve you well here," he responds. "Describe that experience for me. What were the steps you took from the time you first began tilling the soil until you realized a successful harvest?"

I puff on my cigar, pausing to recollect my backyard gardening exploits nearly twenty years past. "Okay, I started by planting two seeds in soil prepared with mulch, rich potting soil, and fertilizer. I watered each seed for about a week. One finally sprouted but was immediately eaten by a bug or a bird or something. The other never came up. So I tried again.

On the second try, both seeds sprouted. Again, a bug ate one and the other just shriveled up and died after a few days. I got pretty frustrated, so I tried a different approach."

"And what was that?"

"This time I dumped the whole package, about fifty seeds, into the garden. After a few days there was a nice little carpet of sprouts. Again, some were eaten and others shriveled up. But so many lived and began to grow that I actually had to thin them out. The remaining plants produced the best cantaloupe I'd ever eaten. In fact, I ended up with so many cantaloupes I was giving them away."

"So, it took you three attempts before you mastered the cantaloupe garden. The first two attempts resulted in frustration, but you persisted. Once you got the hang of it, it became an enjoyable activity rather than a chore."

"I never thought of it that way, but you're right. Even the first couple of tries were still fun. I kept at it because I really enjoyed working in the garden, and I was curious to see what would grow. In fact, each year I got a little better at it. I learned how to grow a lot in a small space, how to time the planting so I'd get an early harvest, and what kind of soil produced sweeter fruit."

"So you continued to grow cantaloupe after that experience?"

"Yeah, every year until I moved out. Once I got the hang of gardening, it was easy. I grew lots of stuff in that garden: zucchini, tomatoes, squash . . . lots of stuff."

"And that is exactly how you'll master the art of hanging out for a living," he responds. "Here's the challenge you're having. At the moment you're in the same place with the relational garden that you were when you first attempted the cantaloupe garden. You simply lack the experience to know for certain that you can build a successful business this way, so it's going to require a combination of faith and persistence. However, the more faith you have the less persistence you'll need. Persistence is necessary in order to develop the proper amount of faith.

As you begin to see the results, which I promise you will, what was once persistence simply becomes habit, a way of life . . . a wonderful, fulfilling, and ultimately quite profitable way of life. Just go into it with the same sense of curiosity and fun you had when you first attempted to grow cantaloupe."

Oscar's comparison of my early gardening experience to the process of developing a referral network makes his point crystal clear. "I get it! I'm hanging out with people because it's fun, I get to help them, and it'll be cool to see what happens. I don't set any expectation that any one individual refers business to me or makes any introductions for me. It's the combined network I develop that will generate business for me. I can't force it. I have to allow it to happen," I say, more to myself than to Oscar.

"You've just beautifully verbalized the concept; however, you have yet to internalize it. Only the actual application of what we've been discussing will accomplish that. That'll require a brief learning curve, just as learning to garden did. But soon you'll relish in a lifestyle that was once a brief period of trial and error."

"You know, I remember some wise adult saying something like that to me when I was first learning to ride a bike. You can't learn to ride without falling down a few times, but once you've got it, you've always got it."

"Riding a bike is a valid analogy. However," he leans toward me with a grin, "learning to hang out for a living requires far less trial and error and carries much less risk of skinned knees and lost teeth."

We both chuckle.

A momentary lull in the conversation allows another concern to pop into my head. "Okay, I've got a question about treating everyone in the relational garden equally."

"Ask away."

"Oscar, my reputation is on the line when I refer or introduce one person to another. I get the part about helping people even if they don't reciprocate. But what if I end up hanging out with someone and discover that they're not somebody I'd be comfortable introducing to my network or referring business to? I don't want to introduce someone to my network whom I don't like or trust myself."

"Excellent point. It's unavoidable that you'll end up hanging out with people who turn out not to be a fit for your network due to what we'll just call a lack of trust. And that, by the way, goes both ways. As sure as the sun will set tonight, you will encounter individuals who don't have the warm-fuzzies for you. But that's one of the primary reasons for hanging out with people, so you can determine if there's the potential for a mutually beneficial networking relationship. So what does one do when a weed appears in the garden?"

"Pull it out."

"There's your answer."

~The Ecology of Hanging Out~

"Now let's talk about the ecology of hanging out with your potential networking partners."

"The ecology of hanging out?"

"Yes. Ever hear of a man by the name of Robert Baden-Powell?"

"No."

"Guess you weren't a Boy Scout."

"No, I never had that opportunity."

"Baden-Powell is known as the father of scouting. In his last message to the scouts he wrote, 'Try and leave this world a little better than you found it.' That concept went on to become a philosophy that has guided not only the scouting movement, but also public land preservation policy worldwide. We're going to take that philosophy one step further. Write this down: leave those you hang out with in a better place than they were before they met with you."

He takes another puff before finishing his thought.

"You leave those you hang out with in a better place by teaching them how to discover their target market and by introducing them to those in your network. The beautiful thing is that, by hanging out with others in this way, you'll also be enriched by their knowledge and experience. That, in itself, is a priceless benefit of hanging out for a living." He looks at the precariously long ash now at the end of his cigar, knocks it into the ashtray, and continues.

~The Hanging Out Conversation~

"So, let's prepare for your meeting tomorrow. I'll be giving you some questions to ask which will serve you well anytime you hang out with a prospective networking partner. Questions designed to give you the information that'll help you help them. These questions will also make every hang out conversation you have interesting, fun, productive, and leave those you hang out with better off than they were before they hung out with you. Ready?"

"Ready!"

"The first two questions are 'How did you get started in your business?' and 'What do you love most about it?' These questions allow the person you're hanging out with to share their story and will tell you what it is that drives them."

I write the questions down and nod my head to let him know I'm ready for the next one.

"Next, have them describe the problem they solve and how. This will require an explanation, just as I had to explain it to you. A good way to do that is to ask them 'What would I hear someone complaining about that would be a signal telling me I should introduce them to you?' If there's time, coach them on coming up with their one sentence description of being the solution to a problem. The example of the mechanic who says 'I make broken cars go' will usually help them come up with it. Use this as an opportunity to share your one sentence description of your solution to a problem.

"Next question is 'How are you different from others in your profession or industry?'

"The next two questions are 'What is the weirdest or funniest thing you've experienced in your business?' and 'What accomplishment are you most proud of?'"

Oscar continues to fire questions at me. I hold my cigar between my teeth while scribbling quickly to keep up.

"'What are your business goals?' Another question along the same lines would be 'What is your exit strategy?'

"'What organized networks do you belong to?' Use examples like chambers of commerce, associations, or service groups.

"Do your best to help the people you hang out with determine their referral market. Start by having them describe their ideal client. Again, you'll need to coach them on this one just as I did with you. Don't let them get away with using terms like *anyone* or *somebody*. Coach them on being specific. Ask 'Who, by nature of their business, would have a network of your ideal client?' and 'Who, by nature of their business, would have a network of those people?' Explain who your eggs, geese, and granny geese are as an example to help them understand. Some people may have difficulty coming up with their target market. But as long as they understand the steps to discovering their target market, you'll always leave those with whom you hang out better off than they were before they met with you."

"Yeah! Learning how to do that was amazing for me, Oscar. But I think I did a better job of figuring it out for my own business when you made it a homework assignment."

"Encourage your networking partners to take the time to do the same thing. Don't hesitate to schedule another time to hang out with them so they can share with you what they came up with. In many cases, you may not have time to get to all of the questions anyway." He taps the ash off his cigar. "In that event, I recommend you keep the primary focus of the conversation on helping them determine their target market. Since most of these people will value your friendship, they'll be happy to get together again to continue the conversation."

~ Conversation Guidelines ~

"Now before you start firing these questions at people, there are a couple of guidelines I recommend that you follow. First, never ask a question you're not prepared to answer yourself. Most people won't be prepared to answer many of these questions. It's your job to help them discover their answers. Your own examples will help them do that, and will also allow them the opportunity to get to know more about you."

"So you're saying I shouldn't ask someone to describe their ideal client, or how they're the solution to a problem, unless I can do the same myself?"

"Right."

"That makes sense."

"The other guideline is to start your conversation by asking permission to take some notes. It's a rare individual who cares enough to actually take notes when first getting to know another person. Therefore, it may take some by surprise when you show up at a meeting waving your notepad full of questions, so best to address it before you begin the conversation. However, you'll find that most people will be extremely impressed that you would take enough interest in them to take notes."

"I know I'd be impressed if someone took that level of interest in me," I interject.

"However, there will occasionally be that individual who objects or voices concern at the idea of you documenting the conversation. In that instance, simply explain that taking notes allows you to be a better connector. Again, most people will be both impressed and appreciative. If they continue to give you any indication that they're uncomfortable by you taking notes, simply put your pen and notepad away, have a casual conversation, and move on. Such a response is an indication that you don't have this person's trust, and that is a valuable thing to discover early on."

"I don't get it. How can it be valuable not to have someone's trust?"

"It's knowing that you don't have their trust that's valuable. The reason is because it tells you that you have likely encountered a weed. If you don't have someone's trust by the time you meet with him or her to hang out, it's unlikely that you'll ever earn his or her trust. Sooner or later you'll encounter such people, but they'll be few and far between."

"So what do I do if they object?"

"You may still be able to serve such a person, but limit the amount of effort you put into it. Just ask questions without writing down their answers, but keep the conversation brief. You both have better things to do than frolic in the weed patch."

~I Don't Have Time~

Oscar's comment about having better things to do stirs a concern that I've had since our second meeting, but have been hesitant to bring up. I examine my cigar, wondering if now is the right time to voice my concern over how much time he's expecting me to spend meeting with people.

"What's on your mind?"

"Oscar, I have a business I'm trying to get started, and a job I have to go to with clients to serve. How the heck do I find the time to hang out and educate others? I've already got like twenty-five people to set appointments with."

"You haven't the time? Poor baby," Oscar sarcastically patronizes me and then rolls his eyes. "Holy smokes kid, can I get you some cheese to go with that whine?"

"C'mon, Oscar. Seriously."

He repositions his body so that he's leaning over the armrest and shoots me a look that tells me I'm about to get a major dressing down. His eyes open wider, and his face turns slightly red.

"Okay, let's get serious. Twenty-five centuries ago I became the largest chariot builder in Babylon and ultimately the most successful merchant in all of Mesopotamia. I obtained my client base exclusively through a method of engaging and serving others using the formula for creating strategic business relationships that we are referring to as hanging out for a living."

His voice grows louder.

"Now I realize many things have changed over the centuries since I started my chariot business. You see, at that time, I was serving as an indentured servant, raising five kids, and supporting a wife. Back then we had no cars. Camels and donkeys were a luxury available only to the privileged. So if I wanted to get anywhere, I walked.

If I needed specialized information, I either traveled to find an elder or journeyed to the caves of Sumer to visit what you might call a library. That trip back and forth took a couple of weeks. Of course, there were no such things as books. All written knowledge was carved into clay tablets. Rummaging through those took a bit more time than instantly retrieving information from your magic gadget there, not to mention a lot more strength!

"We had no postal service or phones or texting or e-mail. I either paid an errand runner to send and receive messages and information, or I delivered the message myself next time I was in the recipients' presence.

"Back then food had to be prepared from scratch—that's after it was cultivated, or slaughtered, or hunted.

"And those are just a few things that used up my time while I built my business. But, back then we had twenty-four hours in a day. Apparently the Earth has sped up, considerably shortening the number of hours in a day." He leans back in his chair, takes a puff on his cigar, and stares at it. "So how long is a day in this century of yours?" he asks sarcastically.

I sit speechless, ashamed of how pathetic my twenty-first century work ethic must seem in comparison.

He gives me a look as if he's expecting me to answer and, after a couple of uncomfortable moments, says, "You have more than enough time to hang out. What you haven't time for is meaningless distractions like television or video games or sitting at your computer discussing what your friends did over the weekend or spending any time watching the mean-spirited bickering, opinion-driven, manufactured melodrama and gossip that you people call news."

"Yes, sir," I reply meekly. I gulp at the realization that I do waste an enormous amount of time on all those things.

"Any other imaginary obstacles getting in your way that you'd care to share, or can we continue?"

Although I'm a bit unnerved by the chewing out I've just received, I'm deeply grateful that Oscar's forcing me to step up and function at a higher level. As gruff and caustic as he can be, I can tell he genuinely cares about me, and my success.

"Please . . . continue."

"Your assignment tonight is to create a way to capture the information you learn about those you hang out with. A referral profile that lists each of the questions you just wrote down, and enough space to capture the answers and contact information of the person you're meeting with. Generate several copies so that you can give it to those you hang out with if they ask for it. Many will be intrigued by such a tool and will ask if they can have access to it."

"I know if someone filled out something like this while learning about me, I'd sure ask for a copy. I'll get it done tonight," I answer while studying the questions Oscar gave me to ask during my hang outs. After some thought, I'm struck by how enormously valuable learning these questions, in fact all of Oscar's coaching, is (including the tongue lashings).

"I don't know how to thank you for teaching me this, Oscar. This stuff is gold. How can I repay you? Is there anything I can do for you?"

"Thanks for asking, because that question brings us to the conclusion of this lesson."

"Huh?"

"The question 'Is there anything I can do for you?' brings us full circle."

"I don't think I'm following you."

"When we began this conversation, you said you were unclear about how you were going to get people to introduce you to those you want to meet?"

"Yeah, and you said I don't. I allow them to."

"Why did you just ask if there's anything you can do for me?"

"Because you've taught me so much. Without your help, I doubt I could have figured this out in my entire lifetime. I want to know what I can do for you."

"In other words, you're grateful for the value you've gained from our conversations?"

"Yeah, big time!"

"And so it will be with those you hang out with. As you tend the relational garden, it will instinctively reciprocate, just as the cantaloupe garden instinctively gives you melons in response to tending the garden. Complete your conversations by asking the question 'How else can I help you with your business?' More often than not, people will complete their response by asking how they can help *you*."

"If someone asked me that, I'd probably be taken off guard and ask them what they meant."

"The question may catch some off guard. Clarify by asking if there's anyone you should be aware of to whom they would like an introduction, or perhaps you could invite them to a networking function, or even arrange a speaking engagement. The point is, more often than not, people will complete their response by asking how they can help *you*. Again, don't expect such a response. Just allow it." With an heir of contentment, Oscar draws on his cigar, staring at the resulting smoke churning upward while I write the final question.

"Anything else I should know before I meet with these folks?"

"Just a suggestion."

"What's that?"

"Didn't you mention that the owners of the medical supply shop are immigrants?"

"Yeah. I think they're Russian."

"What do you know about their culture?"

"Nothing."

"Then may I suggest you bring a small gift to the meeting with you. Nothing fancy, but something they can use."

"You mean like a bottle of wine?"

"Or a box of chocolates, or even a bag of tea from that Tea Zone place. In many cultures such a gesture is considered proper etiquette and will be greatly appreciated."

"Thanks for telling me. I would've just shown up with my notepad and a pen otherwise."

"Which is what they would expect from an American such as yourself. Such a gesture will not offend and may, in fact, make a very nice impression."

"These pointers are awesome, Oscar. But you still haven't answered my question. What can I do for you?" I ask as I set the notepad on the table and retrieve my cigar from the ashtray, which went out some time during our conversation.

The large man blows forth a billow of smoke and leans his head back with a quiet sigh and an expression of enormous self-satisfaction. "There's more for you to learn. At the time my work with you is complete, I'll let you know what you can do for me. Now relax and enjoy your cigar," he says, handing me the lighter.

~If Smoking Is Not Allowed in Heaven, I Shall Not Go~

I relight my cigar and watch as Oscar sits contentedly enjoying his. There are so many things about him that make no sense, but I've just accepted them as part of the mystery of his presence. However, as I watch him puff away, my curiosity grows.

"Can I ask you something that has nothing to do with our lessons?"

"Sure."

"I know there were no such things as cigars in ancient Babylon, so how'd you become such an aficionado?"

With deliberate slowness, Oscar blows a giant cloud of smoke and begins a story. "Back in your late nineteenth century, I had the good fortune of befriending a character whose appetite for life was, let's see, how should I put this . . . formidable." His demeanor suddenly erupts into joviality as fond memories return. "Ha! Sam Clemons, what a pisser that guy was!" he roars.

"Wait a second."

"What?" he asks while chuckling nostalgically.

"Sam Clemons? Samuel Clemons? As in Mark Twain, the author?"

"That's the guy. Though at the time I thought of him as more of a journalist."

"Mark Twain was one of your students? Okay, I gotta hear this one."

"No, he wasn't one of my students. If anything, I was his student," he says fondly. "I ran into him while on assignment in San Francisco. At the time I was giving guidance to an extraordinary woman by the name of Carrie Chapman Catt.

"Carrie was a pivotal figure for the advancement of women's rights in your country. Back then your country was a rather oppressive place to live if you weren't a white, male, protestant non-immigrant. I was working with her to develop a series of speeches to advance the cause of women's suffrage. While there, I ran into Sam, who introduced me to the cigar among other, shall we say, sinful pleasures," he says wagging his eyebrows at me. "'If smoking is not allowed in heaven,' he used to say, 'I shall not go.' Since then, I've made it a point to pick up a few boxes on each assignment before I head back into the teapot. It can be decades before I get another chance to resupply, you know," Oscar says, tapping the ash off his cigar.

"You take boxes of cigars with you into the teapot?" I ask with only partial disbelief. I've pretty much accepted the fact that I'm in the Twilight Zone, so nothing Oscar tells me comes as the surprise it would have a couple of days ago.

"Where else would I keep them?"

"Okay, I'll bite. You smoke 'em in the teapot?"

"Only in the den. I don't want to stink the whole place up, you know."

"Let me get this straight. You have a cigar den . . . in the teapot?" I ask, nonplussed by how absurd the idea sounds.

"Of course. I added it when I had the place redone about a century ago. Has oak paneling, a library, and everything."

"With a humidor, naturally."

"Swiss upright walnut cabinet," he answers nonchalantly, again tapping the ash off his now very short cigar.

One of my fantasies has been to have a cigar den someday. I'm envious of Oscar's description. "Any chance I could get a tour?" I ask, dying of curiosity and at the same time hoping I'm not being rude by inviting myself into Oscar's home.

"I'd love the company, kid, but that's gettin' into that quantum physics thing again. Unfortunately, the place can only handle one occupant at a time."

"Sounds lonely."

"Not at all. I have my books. Besides, time, as you know it, doesn't exist in the teapot. What seems like a couple of days in there can be more than a century out here."

"Curved space-time?" I inquire as I drop my cigar butt in the ashtray.

Oscar answers with a wink, takes a final puff, and adds his to the ashtray. "Well, kid, I've certainly enjoyed our time together today."

"Me too, Oscar. I can't wait for my meeting tomorrow morning." I stand and brush off some ash that has fallen into my lap. "I need to run to the restroom, and then I have to get going. I have class tonight at Slarrefer. Are you going to be here when I get back?" I ask, concerned that he'll disappear on me again.

"Probably not."

"Then when will I see you next?"

"I'll meet you in the field tomorrow. I want to hear how your first hang out went. That'll also be a good opportunity to begin our next lesson."

"What's the next lesson?"

"Networking: where and how to find exactly the right people to hang out with. I'll share an approach with you that I think you'll find to be much more effective than banging on doors."

I reach out to shake his hand goodbye. "I can't wait. Thanks Oscar!"

After a few minutes, I return from the restroom to find my belongings laying in the chair, but no sign of Oscar. The ashtray we'd been using is completely clean. I gather up my notepad and briefcase and check the time: 4:35. It's been only five minutes since I walked into the cigar shop.

Always be prepared to make a sale

I don't GET people to introduce me to their networks. I ALLOW them to.

Always Leave those I hang out with in a better place than they were before they met with me.

1. How did you get started?
2. What do you love most about it?
3. Describe the problem that you solve and how.
4. How are you different from others in the industry?
5. What is the weirdest/funniest thing you've experienced in your business?
6. What accomplishment are you most proud of?
7. What organized networks do you belong to?
8. Describe your ideal client
9. Who would have a network of your idel client?
10. Who, would a have a network of those people?
11. How can I help you with your business? (i.e introduction arrange a speaking engagement, invite to a networking function)

TEN

Nadia and Anton

It's Thursday morning. The Saturn sputters and knocks before going silent, stirring up the butterflies that seem to be ever present in my stomach these days. The dashboard clock tells me it's five minutes before my ten o'clock appointment with Nadia and Anton. I'm excited, though a little nervous, about what the result might be. It occurs to me that the idea of spending valuable sales time in a meeting where the only agenda is to get to know the owners of a business well enough to learn how I can help them build their network would have seemed completely absurd to me just a couple of days ago.

After retrieving a parking sticker from the meter and placing it inside the passenger side window, I lock the car and take a deep breath. Although I'm not here to try to sell an ad, I still feel naked without my briefcase and sample copy of the directory. Armed with only my pen, notepad, a small gift, and three copies of the referral profile I created last night per Oscar's instructions, I enter the shop.

"Good morning, Tyler," Nadia's voice rings out over the jingling of the bell on the door.

"Morning, Nadia, Anton. Good to see you again! How are you both this morning?"

"We are good, very good," Anton answers in his deep, gravelly voice. "How you?"

"I'm doing wonderful, thank you," I reply as I hand Nadia a bag of gift-wrapped chocolate mint tea I picked up at the Tea Zone on the way over. "I brought you something I hope you'll enjoy."

With a gasp she responds, "You're too sweet! Thank you."

"Come, you sit," Anton orders as he places a chair at Nadia's desk, which is covered with a checkered tablecloth.

"Papa is very excited about our meeting. You are the first person who has shown any interest in getting to know us since we moved here," Nadia comments while placing a bowl of assorted olives on the desk. "Have you ever had Armenian coffee?"

I take a seat in the chair Anton offers me. "I can't say that I have."

She pours a thick, black liquid from a carafe into a tiny, ornate porcelain cup on a matching saucer. Without asking, she tosses a sugar cube in and hands the cup and saucer to me as Anton busily places bowls of food on the desk.

With the desk now festooned with meatballs and lentils, an eggplant-yogurt recipe that looks like a pizza gone terribly wrong, salad, the olives, and a dessert plate including baklava, Jordan almonds, and dried fruit, they both join me. I'm overwhelmed at the sight of the unexpected feast.

"We give thanks," Anton announces as he extends his arms to Nadia and me. They each take one of my hands and each other's, bow their heads, and say a brief prayer. Before realizing they're done, I'm startled by Anton barking "Eat! Eat!" Nadia impatiently places a plate in front of me and, with a large spoon, loads it with heaping portions from each of the bowls. I've never been so glad I skipped breakfast.

As we eat, I grow concerned that I could be here all day and decide to get the conversation started. "So tell me about your business. How did you get started in medical supply?"

~I Live American Dream~

Together they tell the story of how Anton brought his wife and daughter to the United States from Armenia twelve years ago. A son, Vartan, had to stay behind to complete his compulsory military service. By the time he had been discharged, the emigration laws had tightened, and he has been unable to obtain a visa to leave Armenia. Nadia tries to hold back tears as she tells the story, lamenting how she has not seen her brother in nearly a decade.

Speaking very slowly and carefully, attempting to pronounce each word correctly, Anton fills in the blanks of the tale.

He was already in his early sixties when the three of them arrived in the United States with less than a thousand dollars. With the help of a cousin he landed a construction job in Glendale, California. At night he delivered pizza, drove a taxi, and when there was time, studied English. He saved every penny he could in order to start his own business. "I live American dream," he says with the pride and appreciation for the American free enterprise system as only an immigrant from an oppressive economic system can.

Having heard that Portland was a more affordable place to live, he researched the area and discovered that the community was underserved in the area of home medical supplies. Just six months ago, he signed a two-year lease on the Pearl District location, and then relocated his wife, Anahit, and Nadia to Oregon.

"My mother is not well and stays upstairs in the attached apartment," Nadia interjects.

Using only his savings, Anton obtained his business and resale licenses and purchased the store inventory. I listen while eating as they both share how difficult it's been to get the business off the ground. "But," Anton says defiantly in his thick accent, "I owe nobody money. I do all myself."

"Papa doesn't believe in borrowing money unless it's a life-or-death situation," Nadia adds.

Humbled by their story, I realize my own circumstances are hardly anything to complain about in comparison. I lay my fork on the plate, retrieve the referral profile from between the sheets of my notepad, and ask, "Do you mind if I take some notes?"

"What this? What you do with this?" Anton asks cynically as he snatches the sheet from my hand.

"It's just a sheet that helps me to keep track of whom I'm networking with," I explain, afraid I've somehow offended them. Anton shows it to Nadia and she translates each item on the sheet for him. With furrowed brows they both look up from the sheet and stare at me quizzically. I remove another copy from between the sheets of my notepad and explain. "I want to collect as many referral profiles as possible. This way I can expand my network by being a connector who helps others expand their networks."

Nadia gives me an intrigued stare.

"You see, at the moment I don't know anyone in need of medical supplies. And honestly, I doubt I'll come across many people who do. But, with your help filling out this sheet, I can probably connect you to people who do know those who might need your service. Is it okay if I fill this out while I ask you these questions about your business?"

Anton's demeanor changes, and he enthusiastically says something to Nadia in Armenian.

"We would be honored," Nadia says as Anton grins and nods his head.

While helping them come up with a one sentence description of the problem they solve, I learn that they specialize in hard-to-find medical supplies and equipment, and will deliver anywhere within a thirty mile radius. "So you make medical supplies easy to get," I suggest in response to her explanation of the problem they solve.

"That is exactly what people need to know about us!" Nadia exclaims. "We should put a sign in the window that says that!" I write the answer *We make medical supplies easy to get* and look up from the notepad to see them both anxiously awaiting my next question. The memory of that early cantaloupe garden comes to mind as I realize how much I'm enjoying this process.

"So what are your goals? Assuming everything goes the way you want, where will your business be in three years?" I continue.

Anton turns to Nadia, letting her know he doesn't quite understand the question. She translates for him, then turns to me and answers, "Papa knows he cannot work much longer. When the business gets a little bigger, we plan to hire some help. Eventually we want to open another store in Beaverton near St. Vincent Medical Center. When my brother finally gets to America, he will run the stores with me. In a few years the business will support us, and we'll have employees running the stores so we don't have to."

Over the next forty-five minutes I help them identify their target market, starting with whom an ideal client might be. They come up with long-term care patients living within seven miles of downtown who have insurance or qualify for Medicare. They both appreciate the analogy of the golden egg and the goose that lays the golden egg and have no problem coming up with three professions that would qualify as potential geese: custodial care providers, home nursing agencies, and Meals on Wheels volunteers. However, both are stumped as I explain the concept of the granny goose being their target market. Using my smart phone I google the words *Oregon home nursing care association*. The search returns the name of an organization: The Oregon Association for Home Care.

Holding my phone over the table so they can both see, I navigate to the membership section of the site and point out the affiliate member option. The site reads

> *Affiliate members are organizations not licensed to provide*
> *care in Oregon, but who provide services or products*
> *to the home-care industry*

Anton slaps his forehead with his palm and again says something to Nadia in Armenian. She then turns to me. "We have heard of this organization, but we had no idea we could be members. This would be a wonderful place to find custodial care providers and home nursing companies. Tyler, this is very helpful," she says with some astonishment. "Thank you!"

Anton again speaks to Nadia, and she then turns to me to translate. "Papa says it seems like we've wasted the last six months trying to find customers. This way of attracting business through relationships is much better than what we've been doing. He says he wishes we'd met you six months ago."

I'm touched by the comment. "Well, I didn't invent this. Someone taught it to me," I respond humbly.

I check the time: 11:15. If I wrap up the conversation now, I'll have plenty of time to make some follow-up calls before the one thirty office meeting I'm required to attend. "Thank you both so much for the wonderful meal. I've really enjoyed our time together. So what can I do to help you with your business?"

"My goodness, you have already done so much!" Nadia exclaims. "You've given us a whole new way of thinking about our business."

Anton grasps my hand with both of his. "Yes, you are good man. Very good man! Thank you."

"Really all I've done is ask you some questions. Is there anything I can do to help you? I know I'll eventually meet people who know those who need your service, and I'll certainly make those introductions. But is there anything else? Do you ever look for opportunities to network with other business people or speak to groups?"

They both look at each other and back at me with blank stares. "No one has asked us that question before. We don't know about networking, and I would be terrified to speak to a group," Nadia replies.

"That's all right. I think I have enough to be of some help to you." I write *Introduce them to custodial care providers, home nursing agencies, and meals on wheels volunteers* on the networking profile sheet, place it between the pages of my notepad and push my chair back. "If you think of anything else, just let me know. My number and e-mail are on my card. Can I at least help you clear the dishes before I go?"

"Wait. Don't we get to learn about you and your business? We want to know how we can help you."

Even though Oscar told me that the networking questions would compel those I hang out with to take an interest in me, I'm taken back by her question.

"Please forgive me. I was so engrossed in learning about you I guess I just forgot to tell you about me. Of course, I'd be happy to show you what I do. May I run out to the car to get my briefcase and a copy of the Yellow Page directory so I can explain how it works and share with you who I'd like to meet?"

"Please, please! We very much want to see," Nadia responds as Anton enthusiastically nods his head.

Networking Profile

Name _Nadia and Anton Gagosian_   Phone _503-555-5540_

Business _Pearl Medical Supply_   Title _Owners_

How did you get started? _Immigrated from Armenia. Relocated to PDX bcause it's more affordable. Found that the community was underserved in the area of home medical supplies. Started business with savings from odd jobs in SoCal._

What do you love most about it? _Helping those in need. Being their own boss. Ability for the family to work together._

Describe the problem that you solve? _We make medical supplies easy to get. (They deliver directly to the patient in sixty minutes or less)_

How are you different from others in your profession/industry? _Home delivery. They can get hard-to-find supplies. Sixty-minute delivery._

Assuming everything goes according to plan, where do you see your business in three years? _Have a second store in Beaverton near St Vincent. Vartan will be working with them. The stores will be run by employees. Enough profit to support the family._

What achievement are you most proud of? _Building the business from scratch. Being debt-free._

What is the funniest or strangest thing that you've seen in your business? _The guy who ordered prosthetic limbs for a Halloween display in his front yard._

What networks do you belong to? _None._

Describe your "ideal" client. _Long-term care patients within 5 miles of downtown who are insured or qualify for medicare._

Who, by nature of their business, would have network of your ideal client? _Custodial care providers. Home nursing agencies. Meals on Wheels volunteers_

Who, by nature of their business, has a network of those people (your target market)? _Oregon Association for Home Care_

How can I help you (i.e. make an introduction, arrange a speaking engagement, media exposure, invite to a networking event) _Introductions to patients and home care providers. Networking events where they can meet potential geese and granny geese_

~We Make Medical Supplies Easy to Get~

Anticipating that I might have a chance to share the directory with Nadia and Anton, I mocked up a sample ad for the medical supply shop last night and pasted it in the medical supply classification of the directory. One of the tricks I was taught in training was how to create a mock ad of a prospect's business and insert it into the book. If a prospect sees how his or her own ad might look in the book, it makes it much more likely that they will buy. Although Oscar made it clear that I shouldn't treat those I hang out with as prospects, but as potential networking partners, my thinking was that they would at least see what an ad for their business might look like. Even if they don't want the ad, it will give them an idea of what's possible so they can tell others.

They both listen intently as I share my story and whom I'm seeking as customers and referral sources. To my delight, Nadia fills in the referral profile sheet while I talk. After showing them the book, highlighting the community features and the restaurant coupon section, I let them thumb through it. They immediately turn to the medical supply classification, see the mock-up, and ask how much. Nadia gasps at the $350 per month price tag. "Do you have anything less expensive?" she asks.

"Of course. Given the type of business you have, I think you'd do just fine with a bold text quarter column listing. In your business, you don't really need to sell people with a big ad. Your potential clients are already in a position of having to buy medical supplies from someone. So the purpose of a bold listing should be to make it easy for those looking for medical supplies to find you."

After explaining the cost of the listing, they instruct me to create the ad copy and fill out a contract. Nadia enthusiastically agrees with my suggestion that the ad header read *We make medical supplies easy to get.*

As I gather my belongings to leave, Anton shakes my hand while Nadia gushes. "Thank you, Tyler. We are very glad we met with you. Thank you so much." Her words leave me feeling like I really made a significant difference.

Although I had no intention of trying to sell an ad, I leave with my second sale, another $545 in annual revenue. Again, not enough to make any significant impact on my sales quota, but this time I feel a real sense of accomplishment. I recall Oscar's words: leave those you hang out with in a better place than they were before they met with you. Mission accomplished.

~What Do I Look Like, the Parking Ticket Fairy?~

So inspired by my experience of hanging out with Nadia and Anton, I'm hardly fazed by the discovery of the parking citation tucked under my windshield wiper when I return to the car. I retrieve the ticket and examine it closely. The forty-five dollar fine for an expired parking sticker pretty much eats up the eight percent commission I'll earn on the meager sale, but it doesn't matter. The experience was so fulfilling that I simply chalk the fine up to the cost of gaining valuable experience.

As I examine the citation, the sound of someone whistling "Wonderful, Wonderful" draws my attention, and I look up to find Oscar leaning against the car, polishing the teapot with his handkerchief.

"I wish you'd take a little better care of this thing. I gotta live here ya know," he says without looking up.

"Oscar!" I exclaim, startled by his sudden appearance. "I'm sorry. I . . . "

"Youse don't see me coming to your place and schmutzin' it all up, do you?" he interrupts.

"I said I'm sorry."

He shakes his head and grumbles under his breath, still intensely focused on polishing the teapot. "So how'd your meeting go?"

"It went pretty much like you'd predicted, but I still wasn't prepared for how appreciative Nadia and Anton were at my interest in them and their business," I answer while walking around the car to unlock the trunk. "And you were right about them wanting to know about me and my business without me even bringing it up. In fact, they bought a bold listing in the book!"

"That, my boy, is only a very small taste of what's yet to come," he answers. He fogs the teapot with his breath and continues polishing as he resumes whistling the old Johnny Mathis tune.

I place my sample directory inside, close the trunk, and step around to join him on the passenger side of the car.

"Now be more careful with this thing, would you?" he admonishes with a stern expression as he hands me the teapot. "How about keeping it someplace safe rather than letting it roll around on the floor of your car?"

Embarrassed and ashamed at my thoughtless treatment of Oscar's home, I open the passenger door and gently place the teapot on the back seat. "I didn't realize, Oscar. I didn't mean to disrespect your place. I'll take it in when I get home tonight."

"Please do," he chastises. "So, you ready to continue our work?"

"Sure. I was headed over to the Tea Zone to get a bite and finish the paperwork for this ad. I might as well leave the car here since I already got a ticket." A thought suddenly occurs to me. "Hey, since you can transcend space and time, is there any chance you can fix this?"

"What do I look like, the parking ticket fairy?" he says with his trademark gruffness, sounding even more like he's from Brooklyn than usual.

"Just asking," I defend. Again, Oscar's coarse nature only strikes me as endearing. I understand that even if it seems he's being hard on me, it's only because he cares, and he's got a job to do.

"I'll see you over there," he says as he starts down the sidewalk. I place the citation back under the wiper and quickly turn to start after him, but he's already gone.

PART
THREE

ELEVEN

Networking 101

I arrive at the Tea Zone to find Oscar already seated at one of the sidewalk tables.

"What took you so long?" he teases.

Almost out of breath, I take a seat, place my briefcase on the table next to a pitcher of iced tea, and, without answering, give him a mock scowl to let him know I'm aware he's trying to give me a hard time. He fills a clear glass teacup and slides it over to me.

"While you were off doing the Watusi, I went ahead and ordered."

I relax into my chair and take a drink of the delicately tropical flavored brew. "Mmm!" I moan at the taste of the unexpectedly delicious beverage. "Is that mango I taste?"

"They call it mango black tea," he answers while looking over the menu. "You know, I think you could spend a month in this place and never get through all of the concoctions listed here."

"Well, this was sure a good call," I reply, bringing the cup to my lips for another sip.

He tosses the menu on the table. "Let's get to it, shall we?"

I retrieve the notepad from my briefcase and turn to a clean page. "Ready."

~ Where to Network ~

Oscar pushes his chair back from the table with his feet, stretches his legs out, and crosses one foot over the other. "Now that you understand the formula for identifying who you want to network with, we're going to shift our focus to finding, and then meeting with them. In other words, networking.

Door-to-door canvassing is an ineffective method of meeting with people for the purpose of building your network marketing business. Today, I'm going to share with you a much more effective way to connect with people." He folds his hands on his belly while rotating his thick thumbs one over the other. "You can network pretty much anywhere other human beings happen to be, but for the purpose of my work with you, we're going to focus on three types of organized networking opportunities: business organizations, business development groups (sometimes known as referral groups), and service clubs."

"Got it," I answer.

"There are a multitude of other places to find people to hang out with, such as alumni associations and community groups, but for my work with you, these three examples will serve us well.

"Today, we're going to focus on business organizations, which include chambers of commerce, industry associations, and trade associations. Such organizations regularly hold networking events like mixers or social events. There's generally no restriction regarding who may attend such functions, but different kinds of events attract different kinds of people. A chamber of commerce mixer, for example, will attract everyone from successful business owners and executives to the part-time network marketer and the gal who makes gift baskets out of her home. An association event, on the other hand, is more likely to attract those whose business is more closely aligned with that particular industry. In any case, the purpose of these events is to meet and become better acquainted with the individuals within that particular business community.

Now, time to pay close attention. If you're going to hang out for a living, you're going to have to become a master networker, and networking events are as good a place as any to start. Ever been to events like that?"

"You mean like a chamber of commerce mixer?"

"Or an association social, an industry conference, or a morning networking forum."

"A few. In one of the network marketing companies I was in we were taught that chamber of commerce mixers were good places to prospect for potential distributors."

An eyebrow goes up, punctuating the subtle expression of disapproval on Oscar's face. "So how exactly did you go about prospecting for people at these events?"

"I was taught to follow the three-foot rule."

"And what is the three-foot rule?"

"Share your opportunity with everyone who gets within three feet of you."

He places an elbow on the armrest of his chair, rests his cheek in the palm of his hand, and with a sigh asks, "So how'd that work out for you?"

"I didn't have much success. It was like the people there were too important to talk to me, like I wasn't part of their clique. I haven't been to one of those events in quite a while. They're just too uncomfortable and not very productive."

Oscar taps his index finger against his cheek. "So you went there to, in your words, share your opportunity with anyone who got within three feet of you, and you were put off to discover that no one wanted to get within three feet of you?"

"Well, I didn't see it that way at the time, but when you say it like that, it does seem ridiculous," I answer sheepishly.

His expression turns to sympathy. "Your experience isn't uncommon for the uninitiated networker. You see, my boy, it wasn't the event that was unproductive, but rather your approach. However, mistakes are how we learn. Give yourself credit for at least recognizing that you learned what doesn't work. From now on you'll have an entirely different experience," he says, pointing a stern finger at me, "if you follow my instructions."

"I'm listening!" I answer enthusiastically, excited by the idea of learning how to be among the well connected.

"Your purpose for attending any networking event should be to become better acquainted with other members of that business community, not to sell or prospect. If you're there to recruit or sell you'll always have an unfulfilling experience, even if you do eventually make a sale."

"I don't get it, Oscar. Other than the free food, what's the point of going to a networking event if it's not to drum up some business?" I argue.

~Tilling the Soil~

"Allow me to answer your question by returning to our gardening analogy. What's the point of growing a vegetable garden?"

"To harvest vegetables, I suppose."

"Is there any point in going into a garden if it hasn't yet produced any vegetables?"

"I don't think I understand the question."

"A garden starts with a bare piece of ground, does it not?"

"Well, yeah."

"What would you expect to harvest from a bare piece of ground?"

"I wouldn't expect to harvest anything. You have to grow the garden before you get vegetables."

"Be more specific."

"You need to prepare the soil, plant the seeds, water, weed, and all that kind of stuff. You also have to allow enough time for the vegetables to grow."

"So, according to you, the purpose of being in a vegetable garden that does not yet offer a harvest is to do the gardening?"

"Of course."

"Showing up at a networking event with the intention of drumming up some business, as you put it, is like walking onto the bare piece of ground for the purpose of harvesting vegetables. One does not earn the right to a harvest without first doing the gardening.

"Let's pursue the metaphor a little further. You live in an age when you buy produce grown almost anywhere in the world from the local store. So why would anyone go to the trouble of gardening?"

"Aside from the quality of home-grown produce, I think the reason anyone gardens is for the enjoyment of gardening."

"Exactly!" Oscar exclaims, throwing his big arms into the air. "And that, my boy, should be the reason you attend a networking event, to support the event, and to enjoy the process. Revenue will eventually occur as a result, just as vegetables eventually occur as a result of gardening. And just as you must serve the garden before earning a harvest, you must show up at a networking event in service to the networking process. By showing up with a philosophy of service, you'll find that there is actually more fulfillment in the process of networking than there is in the harvest. Networking is far more profitable and enjoyable when your purpose is to find and nurture relationships rather than selling stuff to people."

"I think I'm getting it," I reply, still trying to digest this completely new way of thinking about networking.

"Thinking you've got it won't get you a passing grade in the class, kid. We're going to make sure you have got it. To do that, I'm going to have you experience the networking process firsthand, which is going to require some fieldwork."

"Fieldwork?"

"Yes. Time to do some actual networking so you can develop your networking skills. Let's start by having you visit a local networking event. You told me that, in the past, you showed up at chamber mixers to prospect for new clients and recruits . . . and for some free food," he says with a roll of his eyes. "This time you'll be attending with a specific purpose that reflects the ninety/ten rule for hanging out for a living."

"Ninety/ten rule?"

Oscar gives me a look that tells me I should know what he's talking about. "Remember, hanging out for a living is only possible if . . . "

"One does so in service to others," I say in unison with him, recalling the fundamental principal that he made such a strong point of impressing upon me in our earlier lesson.

"And if you must ask, then it's a good time to remind you that hanging out for a living is ten percent strategy and ninety percent philosophy, the philosophy of serving others."

"And the philosophy is the most important part," I affirm.

"Right. There is a networking strategy," he says, laying open his left hand, "and a networking philosophy." He completes the sentence making the same gesture with his right hand. "I can teach you the strategy, but that strategy must be practiced with the right philosophy." He cups his hands together to complete his illustration.

~Networking Strategy~

"So let's see how well you've learned so far. What's your purpose for attending a networking event?"

"To find people to build relationships with?"

"Correct, the purpose is to build relationships, not to sell anyone your company's financial services, or to prospect for other representatives for your company. Now, if you're going to be hanging out for a living, you'd better be hanging out with the right people. Since your intention is to build a Slipperyfur distributorship, who specifically are you looking to build relationships with?"

I've given up on getting Oscar to pronounce Slarrefer correctly, so I let it go. Still getting used to this way of thinking, it takes me a moment to respond. "Oh, of course, my geese and granny geese: CPAs, estate planning attorneys, and payroll service sales reps."

"Very good! And how will you find them at the event?"

"Shake everyone's hand until I find someone who's either a CPA, estate planning attorney, or a payroll company rep?" I venture apprehensively with a shrug of my shoulders.

"Meeting everyone at an event in the hope that you eventually come across whomever you're looking to meet would be the needle-in-the-haystack approach. If there are a hundred people in attendance, but only one or two of them qualify to be your goose or granny goose, chances are you'll never meet them. Better to know exactly whom you're going to meet in advance."

"Oscar, I'm not psychic. How can I possibly know in advance if any estate planning attorneys or payroll service reps are going to show up at a networking event?"

He raises his eyebrows and shoots me a look that says the answer is as obvious as the nose on my face. "Try asking."

I have no idea what he's talking about and tell him so by returning his look with a blank expression.

"Okay," he says, letting out a sigh. "First I'll tell you, and then I'll show you. Write this down.

"Step one: find a local networking event. I recommend starting with a chamber mixer or an industry association event that will attract a broad range of professionals.

"Step two: call ahead to ask if you can attend the event. Ask whomever you speak to if they would be willing to introduce you around since this is your first time there and you won't know anyone. As a representative of the organization, they will, of course, be happy to do so.

"Step three: tell that person whom you want to be introduced to. Ask to be introduced to those particular people.

"Step four: go to the event and allow this individual to introduce you to exactly the people you want to meet."

"Oscar, this is brilliant. And it's so simple," I respond, feverishly taking notes.

"It is simple, and I think you'll find it to be a lot of fun too. You're going to discover that attending such an event with the right purpose is just like going to a party and meeting new friends. Ultimately, that's why you're going there, to cultivate friendships. In particular, friendships with people whom you can relate to, whose professions you can appreciate, and, of course, those who can relate to your financial services venture and who would therefore be interested in what you're up to."

"I have to admit it makes sense. I know I'd rather meet people who are genuinely interested in me than I would people who I suspect are only interested in selling me something."

"Everyone would."

"You know, Oscar, I've always wanted people to be interested in me and my business, but until now, it never occurred to me to attract them by being someone who is interested in them."

"Well, from now on you're going to be such a person, and in so doing, you will attract such people."

"So where do I start?"

"Start by finding a networking event. You got that fancy gizmo there. If you can find a business coach for a plumbing contractor with that thing, you should have no problem finding a networking event."

"Of course!" I exclaim. "Let's use my laptop, though. It's easier to see."

I remove my laptop from the briefcase, scoot my chair to Oscar's side of the table, and sidle up next to him so we can both see. I tap the words *Portland networking* into the search field. An organization called the Portland Business Alliance pops up in the search results. The name intrigues me. I click the link, which opens a website that describes the alliance as an organization that came to be as the result of a merger between the nearly one-hundred-fifty-year-old Portland Chamber of Commerce and an organization called the Association for Portland Progress. Oscar and I look through the website and discover a link for upcoming events.

"Let's see what they've got going on," he says, pointing at the events link. I click the link, and a menu of upcoming events drops down along with a message: *Attendance at Alliance events is a benefit of membership. It is Alliance policy to welcome first-time non-members to attend up to two networking events.*

"I'd be a first-time non-member," I say enthusiastically to my supernal friend.

"Keep going," he says impatiently, pointing at the screen. The website lists several events, one in particular catches both our attention.

Business After Hours

Business After Hours offers an opportunity to create new business relationships by networking in a relaxed setting that offers delicious appetizers, door prizes, and refreshments from a no-host bar.

Oscar points to the event description and taps on the screen. "*That* is a networking event. Let's find out what the deal is."

The link informs us that the next event is being held this evening. "Hey look, Oscar, it's tonight . . . at the Oregon Culinary Institute! You sure I can't show up for the free food?" I joke.

He pats me on the back. "I'm sure you'll be able to have your share and do your networking as well. Just make sure you keep your priorities straight while you're there."

"I will," I answer, returning my attention to the screen. "Look, there's a number to call."

Oscar waves his fingers at my computer, gesturing for me to get on with it. As I make the call, the expression on his face tells me he's looking forward to seeing what will transpire. A young man answers and transfers me to the membership department. The first ring is cut short by a voice.

"This is Peggy."

"Hi Peggy, my name is Tyler Cirella. I understand you're the person to talk to about attending the networking events."

"I'm the one!"

"I was just browsing your website, and I see there's something called Business After Hours tonight."

"Yes, from five to seven at the Oregon Culinary Institute in Goose Hollow. Would you like to join us?"

"Yes, I think I would!"

"Have you ever been to an alliance event before?"

"No. In fact, until a couple of minutes ago, I'd never heard of the alliance."

"In that case, you're welcome to come as my guest."

"That'd be great!"

"So what is your business, Tyler?"

"I'm just getting started as an independent agent with Slarrefer Mutual."

"I'm not familiar with them. What do you do there?"

"We offer life and long-term care insurance, as well as financial planning resources and education. I'm pre-contract with the company, which means I can work part-time and earn commissions, but I just don't actually get paid until I complete my training and hit my probationary quota. I'm working with a business mentor who suggested I start building business relationships right away rather than wait until I've completed my training." I look at Oscar's face for some kind of expression that tells me I'm saying the right things.

"Sounds like you've got a very good mentor."

"Oh, he's one of a kind all right. So how many people show up to these things, Peggy?"

"As of right now, we have eighty-three people registered."

"Wow, sounds like a good sized group."

"It is. That's partly because it's at the Culinary Institute this month. You'd be surprised how many people will show up just for the free food."

"Really, I never would have guessed," I reply uncomfortably.

"Tyler, let me get your information, and we'll have a name tag waiting at the door for you."

I finish spelling my last name and ask, "Peggy, since I won't know anyone there, would you be willing to introduce me around?"

"I'd be happy to, Tyler."

"Great! I'm really interested in building connections with estate planning attorneys, financial advisors, and payroll service representatives. Do you know if anyone like that will be there?"

"I can think of three or four people right off the bat. I'd be happy to introduce you. Can you arrive a few minutes early so we can connect?"

"Sure."

"If I'm not at the registration table when you get there, just ask for me. And be sure to bring plenty of business cards. I can't wait to meet you!"

"Thanks, Peggy. I can't wait to meet you too. See you tonight. Bye."

After ending the call, I give Oscar a stare and nod my head to show my amazement. "She said they have eighty-three people registered to attend, and she knows three or four who would be my geese and granny geese! Oscar, you just saved me from having to collect eighty-three business cards to meet the three or four people I really want to meet."

"Does your pal Oscar know his stuff?" he asks proudly, holding his hand up to me in a high-five gesture.

"Oscar knows his stuff!" I declare as we slap palms. "But now I've got a problem."

"Now what?"

"She told me to bring business cards. I don't have any business cards for Slarrefer yet. Oscar, if I show up at a networking function for the first time without business cards, I'll be like the guy who forgot to put on his pants," I say in a panic.

"You worry too much. It's not that bad."

"It's not?"

"No. Showing up at a networking event without business cards is a sin, but it's only a minor sin. Remember, you're showing up there as a networker, not a salesperson. Therefore, it's far more important that you collect business cards from those you want to develop business relationships with than it is to hand out yours. In fact, someone who passes out more than half a dozen business cards at any event is probably not networking very effectively."

"Oscar, I've always been taught that you were supposed to hand out as many business cards as you could at an event."

"How much business have you generated by handing out your business card?"

"You don't generate business by handing out a card Oscar, it's like . . . it's like branding. If people see it enough, it builds credibility."

He gives me a vacant yet knowing expression that says he knows I don't even believe that.

"Okay, but it's what everyone does, and it's what I've always done. So what's the point of having business cards if I shouldn't hand them out?"

Oscar shakes his head at me like I told him I couldn't find a pair of glasses that I'd forgotten I was wearing. "Let's explore this a bit, shall we?" he says with a tone that tells me I'm going to feel like an idiot in just a minute. "Have you been to an event where you collected lots of business cards?"

"Sure."

"What did you do with them?"

"Well, when I got home I looked through them and . . . ."

"Yes?" he says expectantly.

"I followed up with an e-mail letting them know that if they'd like to find out how my service might benefit them, I'd be happy to talk with them."

"My, how generous of you. I'm sure you were bombarded with eager responses," he responds sarcastically.

"No, I wasn't. Okay, I get it. I was hunting."

"Yes you were, and everyone who received that message from you saw through that sheep costume of an e-mail to the wolf who was behind it. So, then what did you do with those cards?"

"Well I . . . I guess I . . . I guess I put them on the dresser and then after a couple of days tossed them," I stammer with a sigh.

"And do you seriously think people are coveting your business card like it's some kind of collector's item when they empty their pockets after an event?"

"I never thought about it."

"If each of your business cards cost ten dollars, would you hand them out so freely?"

"No, I guess I wouldn't."

"Your business card is an extension of you. You give away a piece of yourself each time you hand one out. If you know that most of them will end up in the trash, what does that say about your self-worth?"

"I never thought about it like that. So what am I supposed to do?"

"Give your business card only when it is asked for. If you meet someone that you want to follow up with, get theirs and then ask them if they would like one of yours. Tonight I want you to consider the idea that you're your own best business card by being the kind of person you'd like to run into there. If someone asks for your card, just say you're all out, but you'd love to get theirs."

"If you say so," I reply uncomfortably.

~Networking Event Dos and Don'ts~

A light breeze picks up, sending the pages of my notepad fluttering and a napkin airborne, which Oscar deftly snatches before it gets away. He places it under his teacup and continues. "Now let's talk about how to conduct yourself at the event, which leads us to the philosophical purpose for attending, which is to contribute to this event by making it better than it would have been had you not been there."

"How do I do that?"

"By giving away that which you seek. You just asked the gal on the phone to introduce you around to people at the mixer. While you're there, you should do the same."

"But I don't know anyone there."

"You know this Peggy person."

"Oscar, I just had a two-minute phone conversation with her, I don't even know what she looks like."

"You'll know what she looks like when you meet her. Now quit yer blubbering and listen. What's Peggy's job?"

"The website says she's a business development manager."

"That's a fancy way of saying that her job is to find new members for the alliance, which is why your call was directed to her. At events such as these, all sorts of people show up, members and non-members alike. You will, almost certainly, run into another non-member such as yourself. If they haven't already spoken with another business development whatever-you-call-it, make a point of introducing that person to Peggy."

"Yeah, I could do that."

"The point is that by enhancing the experience of others, you'll make the event better than if you hadn't been there."

He refills his teacup, leans back with a sigh, and gives me a thoughtful stare. "Ever been to an event where you didn't know a soul, an event where you ended up milling about without anyone paying any attention to you because they were all engaged in conversations? It felt rude to interrupt, so you wandered about awkwardly hoping to find someone to talk to, and before long you found yourself chatting with the bartender just to keep from feeling like the bacon sandwich at a bar mitzvah?"

"I sure have. I think the main reason I've avoided attending events like these is because that's exactly what my experience was like."

"Think back to an event where you didn't know anyone and you felt out of place. Concentrate. What was the one thing you wanted to happen?"

I close my eyes to recollect my last networking experience. I open them and answer, "I guess I just wanted someone to talk to."

"Then, in the spirit of giving away what it is that you want, make it a point to seek out those who appear lost or lonely. For as sure as the sun will set this evening, there'll be a lost and lonely soul at that event tonight wishing they had someone to talk to. Making that person feel welcome is one small way to make an event better than it would have been if you had not been there."

"But what if they're not who I'm looking to meet? What do I say to them?"

"The same thing you would say to the person who's exactly whom you want to meet. Remember, the event is an unplowed field of relational possibilities. Your job is to till the soil and plant the seeds, not to judge which ones will produce. Only by treating all the seeds with the proper care do you deserve a harvest. Remember, all are created equal in the eyes of creation. Therefore, as a matter of practice, you should treat everyone at the event equally."

"Just so you know, Oscar, I'm not very religious. You're beginning to sound kind of biblical."

"I'm not here to influence your spiritual path. However, The Good Book is rife with divine wisdom. To paraphrase the words of the Kristos, according to Matthew, 'As you do unto the least of my brethren, so you do unto me,' meaning everyone is equal in the eyes of the Lord, and so it is in the world of hanging out for a living. That includes the socially awkward individuals you may encounter standing by themselves at business events like the one you'll be attending tonight."

"I think I understand. Pretend it's my party and the people there are just guests I haven't met yet."

Oscar pats me on the shoulder. "That would be an excellent attitude to show up with."

A streetcar rumbles past, forcing a break in the conversation. I take the opportunity to refill my cup. As I do, Oscar's expression becomes slightly more serious.

"Next pointer: it's important that you be respectful of your time and the time of others at the event. Spend no more than five minutes with any one individual. A networking event isn't the place to hang out. It's the place to discover new relationships. Answer questions without hogging the conversation, and be sure to ask good questions."

"Good questions?"

"Yes. Questions designed to let the person you're speaking to know you're genuinely interested in them, and at the same time help you determine if they're someone you'd like to get to know better. Questions like 'How did you get started?' and 'What do you like most about doing that?' You can find out a lot about a person in less than five minutes. Any conversation that's so good it takes longer than that needs to be continued one-on-one at a later time.

"Once you determine that you've found someone to network with, simply end the conversation with 'I'm interested in finding out more about your business and discovering how we might network together. Would you be open to getting together for coffee?'"

"That's great, Oscar! If they say yes, I've actually got someone who wants to hang out. If they say no, then I haven't wasted any time."

"Now you're gettin' it. This initial invitation to hang out is the first of three very important steps to successfully scheduling the appointment." He takes another look at the website. "According to this, it's a two-hour event. You should have plenty of time to meet those you want to be introduced to, as well as mingle with others and even get something to eat."

"I like this. It takes the pressure off trying to meet everyone, and I'll actually be able to enjoy myself. I can already tell I'm going to enjoy gardening a lot more than hunting!"

"That's my boy. Now that we've covered the dos, let's go over the don'ts.

"Don't hand out promotional materials, like brochures. Such behavior would instantly reveal you as a hunter. No one comes to a networking event to collect brochures."

"Got it," I answer as I write my notes.

"Don't, under any circumstances, add anyone to an e-mail distribution list without their expressed consent."

"Yeah, I already learned that lesson. Remember I said I sent a bulk e-mail to the people I met at a networking event?"

"Yes?"

"Then it happened to me. I had to get rid of an e-mail address after attending just one networking event a couple of years ago. I began getting all these newsletters I didn't subscribe to, and repeated e-mails from people telling me they'd be happy to discuss how their product or service could 'benefit' me," I reply with a roll of my eyes. "I finally figured out it was all coming from people I met at that one event."

"You've just revealed another good reason for not handing out your business card so freely," Oscar says with a grin. "In any case, only send an e-mail to someone to communicate directly with that individual regarding your intention to foster a relationship, not sell or mass market."

I nod my head in agreement.

"This next don't is especially important for you, my boy. Do not promote more than one business at a networking event. You're going to have to avoid the temptation to mention your day job with Yellow Page USA, even if you run into that ideal Yellow Page client. Doing so would be very bad form and highly counterproductive."

"But Oscar, I'm three weeks away from losing my job. You're telling me that if I come across a prospective Yellow Page client tonight, I can't mention it to them?"

"Ah-ah-ah," Oscar interrupts, holding his palm out to me. "No arguments on this one. Imagine you were to meet someone at a networking event who showed up as, oh, let's say a realtor, for example."

"Okay."

"During the conversation he mentions that he also sells insurance. He tells you that he can hook you up with a sweet deal on a life insurance. What would be your reaction?"

I ponder the question before answering. "Well, I guess I'd be confused about what business he's actually in. Wow, you're right. I wouldn't trust him to do either job."

"Explain why."

"I'd just assume he's promoting two professions because he's probably not very good at either."

Oscar nods his head, letting me know I've answered correctly.

~Brush Your Teeth~

"One more thing before we move on."

"What's that?"

"Brush your teeth."

"Brush my teeth?"

"Yes, brush your teeth and gargle before you go to the mixer, and bring some breath mints with you."

Embarrassed and shocked I breathe on my palm to see if I can detect anything offensive. "I had no idea, Oscar. I brushed my teeth this morning."

"No, no," he corrects. "As a matter of practice, always brush your teeth and gargle before you show up at an event. And bring some breath mints with you."

I laugh, relieved that I'm not personally sharing any offensive odors. "You had me scared there, Oscar. I was ready to run to the dentist for a tongue scraping."

"Nah, you're fine. But when you're in another's space at an event, a little stale breath can distract them from hearing a single word you say."

"Good advice. I've been in conversations with people with barn breath, and you're right, I didn't hear a single word they were saying," I reply while retrieving a breath strip from my pocket, just in case, prompting a chuckle from Oscar.

"Now remember, this is just your first time. Have fun. Enjoy yourself. As you build your network and become more involved with organizations such as this, you'll become increasingly better equipped to help others. By allowing this Peggy gal to help you, you're simply empowering yourself to help others."

"This is good stuff, Oscar."

"It's the only kind of stuff I got," he says bringing his teacup to his lips.

Networking

- Find a local networking event (i.e. chamber mixer or industry association event).

- Call to ask if I can attend and if they'll introduce me around. Tell them who I want to be introduced to (i.e. CPAs, estate planning attorneys).

- Go to the event to get introduced to exactly the people I want to meet!

Oregon Culinary
Institute in
Goose Hollow – 5:PM
Ask for Peggy

Give my business card only when it's asked for.

Make the event better than it would have been if I hadn't been there.
    - Make introductions
    - Talk to people who look lost

Pretend it's my party!

- Spend no more than 5 min. with anyone.
- No brochures
- No e-mail blasts

Breath mints!

~*Follow Up*~

"Can I get you anything else?" a waitress asks as she places the check on the table. We look at each other and back at her.

"No thanks," I reply.

As she clears the table, Oscar continues. "Now that you know how to conduct yourself at an event, let's discuss what you must do after the event. It's critically important that you effectively follow up with those you want to hang out with. Now it's unavoidable that you'll have business cards of those you don't want to hang out with shoved into your hand. To protect your time and your sanity, be sure you don't get them mixed up with those you do want to hang out with. Choose a pocket for the keepers and a pocket for the others. Immediately after the event, take the keepers and start writing."

"Start writing what?"

"Follow-up notes."

I dread the thought of what I think Oscar is suggesting. "Follow-up notes? You mean a text message or an e-mail, right?"

"No, I mean a hand-written note. Do you want to chase people who ignore your offer to hang out, or do you want to set appointments with people who enthusiastically accept your invitation?"

"Accept my invitation, of course."

"Then pipe down and listen," he scolds affectionately. "You're going to follow up using a two-step method. The first step is to send a physical note to those that you want to meet with. It's important that you get this into the mail as soon as possible, immediately after the event would be best. The sooner they receive it, the better."

"This isn't the first time I've heard this, Oscar," I reply while turning to a fresh page on my notepad. "I remember reading a book by Tom Hopkins that said most of his sales were generated by referral, and that he attributed his success to the habit his mother got him into of sending out handwritten greeting cards. And Joe Girard wrote a book a called *How To Sell Anything To Anyone* where he said following up with cards was key to his success. So I'm familiar with this process, but I never bothered to do it because it always sounded so time-consuming," I say, with an exasperated sigh as I write *BUY GREETING CARDS* in large letters on my notepad.

"Well now you're going to do it, and I guarantee that the results will far outweigh the effort.

"The second step is to call each person no later than the following day to set up an appointment. Of course, you'll end up getting a voicemail about half of the time." He leans forward and lowers his voice like he's telling me some secret he doesn't want anyone else to hear. "You're going to discover that roughly two-thirds of those you leave a message for won't return your call, even though you told them to expect your call.

Don't read anything into that lack of response. People's attention spans are simply spread too thin in this day and age, and it's easy to lose track of voicemails. You may be astonished to find, however, that those who don't return your call immediately will do so as soon as they get your card in the mail."

"Really?"

"Really. Now, remember that effectively setting up an appointment to hang out begins with that initial conversation at the networking event. Sending a card and then calling are steps two and three to the appointment-setting process. Step one is the conversation you have at the networking event when offering to get together to learn more about each other's business. The call and the card will have little intended effect if you haven't set the expectation for them to hear from you to set a time to hang out.

By following these three steps, you'll have no problem successfully setting an appointment with about nine out of ten people. In the rare event that you don't receive a call back from someone within about five days, make another call or send an e-mail reminding them of your discussion at the event about getting together to find out more about them and their business. If they still don't respond, then they've probably just been sidetracked by a personal or professional issue that prevents them from getting back to you. Of course, it's possible that you misread this person and they really don't want to meet with you, but that's unlikely. In either case, let it lie. If it's the former, they'll respond when they're able, and if it's the latter, chasing them won't turn them into someone who wants to meet with you."

I'm writing furiously to get Oscar's process down. I finish and check the time. It's one. "Oscar, I need to get to the office soon for a meeting."

"Tell you what. Let's get back together tonight after the mixer to continue the conversation. You can give me a full report then."

"Okay. Where should we meet?"

There's a bookstore here in town with quite the reputation that I've been meaning to visit during this assignment, and I understand that it has a coffee shop."

"You must mean the coffee room in Powell's."

"That's the place."

"That's a great idea, Oscar. They sell greeting cards there too. Meet you at seven thirty?"

"Seven thirty it is. Bring the business cards of the people you want to follow up with, and we'll discuss how to effectively word the cards."

"I'll be there. Oh, and one more thing, Oscar," I say as I stand to leave.

"What's that?"

"Let me be the one who disappears this time."

He shrugs his huge shoulders and replies, "As you wish."

I pick up my notepad and head off toward the car.

~Glenn~

Upon arriving at the Saturn, I remove the parking ticket from the windshield and walk around the car to unlock the door.

"Hey, Tyler!"

I turn around to see a coworker, Glenn, approaching. He's my least favorite person in the office. Glenn takes a perverse delight in watching newer reps struggle, and he knows I'm on thin ice with Yellow Page USA. Every time he sees me, he makes sure to let me know about his latest sale. Though considered to be one of the top producers in the office, he has a very high number of contract disputes and customer complaints against him.

"Hey, Glen, what're you doing here?" I ask lethargically, wondering why he's in my territory and hoping this encounter doesn't take long.

"Oh, I was just down the block knocking out a twelve-thousand-dollar renewal," he says condescendingly. "What about you?"

"I just signed up this medical supply shop."

"What'd they buy?"

"A bold listing."

"A bold listing? I won't even touch those. If it's not at least five hundred a month, I won't waste my time."

I've heard enough. I climb into the car, start the engine, roll down the window and reply, "Sometimes a bold listing is what's best for the customer, Glenn."

He puts his hand on the roof of the car and leans into the window. "You know what your problem is, Cirella? You think you work for the customer. We work for the company, not the advertisers. Remember, buyers are liars. They're all cheapskates who don't want to spend any money, so they tell you all they can afford is a bold listing. If this'd been my account, I could've squeezed 'em for at least a quarter page."

"I'd love to stay and chat, Glenn, but have to be at the office at one thirty."

With a dismissive snicker he replies, "Me too. I've got real sales to make."

I pull away from the curb and mutter, "I can't stand that guy."

TWELVE

The Mixer

The pneumatic doors of the MAX light rail train open with a loud hiss, dropping me off at the Goose Hollow station. Limited street parking and one-way streets can make pedestrian-friendly downtown Portland a very frustrating place to navigate in a car, so I left the Saturn in a lot near Powell's bookstore, took the streetcar to the MAX line, and then the MAX to Goose Hollow—about a twenty-five minute journey in all. From here it's just a short one-block walk to the Oregon Culinary Institute.

It's ten minutes before five as I open the door to the restaurant and am greeted by the tantalizing aromas of garlic roasting, bacon frying, and fresh-baked bread. *You didn't come here for the food*, I have to remind myself.

The Culinary Institute is a cooking school that operates the restaurant out of their Jefferson Street facility. The restaurant is really a classroom in disguise. It's an open space filled with natural light during the day from the floor to ceiling windows that wrap around this corner of the building. The windows also provide a largely unobstructed view of the comings and goings of the neighborhood. An open kitchen allows diners to observe the students preparing meals under the close supervision of the institute faculty.

"May I get your name?" the young woman seated behind the check-in table asks.

"Tyler Cirella. I'm a guest of Peggy's."

"Yes, here you are," she says, crossing a line through my name on the guest list. "Peggy's expecting you."

"Peg, your guest's here," she calls across the restaurant space, waving her hand to get Peggy's attention. "Here's your nametag, Tyler. Have a wonderful time." I notice her nametag says Sandra.

"Thanks, Sandra. I'm sure I will."

In a moment, a perky fifty-something blonde, followed by a short, smartly dressed man, approaches and embraces my hand with both of hers. "You must be Tyler."

"I am. Pleasure to meet you, Peggy."

"Tyler, I have someone I want you to meet." She motions for the gentleman to join us. "Tyler, this is Brent Walker. He owns Krowten Payroll Service."

"Pleasure to meet you, Brent."

"Nice to meet you, too. So tell me, Tyler, what do you do?"

"I'm with Slarrefer Mutual. I help CPAs, bookkeepers, and tax specialists bring financial security to their clients."

"I've heard of Slarrefer, but I'm not that familiar with them. However, my company collaborates heavily with CPAs, bookkeepers, and tax specialists. How does Slarrefer work with them?"

After briefly explaining Slarrefer's services, my freshman role with the company, and why I asked Peggy for an introduction to someone in the payroll industry, I make a point of turning the conversation back to Brent. Within moments I realize he's exactly the kind of person I'd like to get to know better.

"Brent, I'd be interested in finding out more about you and Krowten Payroll. Would you be open to getting together for coffee so we can see how we might network together?"

"I was just going to suggest the same thing."

"Great. Can I get your card?"

"Sure," he says, pulling one from a metal business card case. "Can I get one of yours?"

"I'm afraid they're still being printed," I reply. "But I promise I'll be in touch with you." I examine his card and see there's no mailing address. "Could I get your mailing address, Brent? I always like to follow up with a note in the mail."

He shrugs his shoulders. "Sure."

"All right if I give you call tomorrow to set up a time to get together?" I ask as I write his address on the back of his card.

"Absolutely. If I'm not available, just leave a message with my secretary."

"Great. I look forward to getting to know you more, Brent."

"As do I you, Tyler. It was a pleasure to meet you."

We shake hands, and I turn my attention to discover the restaurant is now crowded with people attending the mixer. A young man approaches offering a platter of drinks and hors d'oeuvres. I take one of the bacon-wrapped oysters and a glass of merlot, and then notice Peggy across the room waving to get my attention. Quickly devouring the appetizer, I make way through the crowd.

"Tyler, this is Cheryl. She's an estate planning attorney with Goldman, Snyder and Price."

I wipe my free hand with a napkin and introduce myself to Cheryl. Within a few minutes, I have another card and a promise to schedule a coffee meeting.

Another server passes by with a platter of savory pastries, ground rosemary infused lamb in a delicate phyllo dough crust. I remove one from the platter and take a bite. As I do, I notice a short, overweight woman standing alone by the window. She's holding onto a glass tightly with both hands, staring into the crowd and looking very uncomfortable behind a pair of thick-framed Coke-bottle glasses. I seize the opportunity to make the event better than it would have been had I not been here. I walk over, see the name Paula on her nametag, extend my hand, and introduce myself. "Hi, Paula. I'm Tyler."

The stunned expression on her face tells me that she was probably praying nobody would talk to her. "Hello," she replies with a peep that I can barely hear over the din of the crowd.

"So what do you do?"

"Bookkeeping," she answers, while staring into her glass.

I can see this conversation is going nowhere fast, but forge ahead. "So, are you a member of the alliance?"

"No. My boss sent me here. She wanted me to find out if this would be a good event to find new clients."

"Are you part of a bookkeeping firm?"

"Yes," she squeaks, her eyes darting everywhere except at me as she nervously sips a soft drink.

"So, what kind of clients are you looking for?"

"Oh, anyone who needs bookkeeping."

I'm dying here, and what's worse is she's probably saying the same thing to herself. I try a different approach. "What kind of clients does your firm currently work with?"

"Oh, mostly small manufacturing companies."

Finally, I'm getting somewhere. "Is that the only kind of clients you'd like to find, or are you interested in serving other industries?"

"My boss says she wants to bring on some construction companies too."

"Have you spoken to any of the alliance staff about that?"

"No, I don't know anyone here."

"May I introduce you to someone who might be able to help you?"

Her face brightens, and she actually looks at me. "You would do that?"

"Sure. Wait right here."

I make my way through the crowd to Peggy and explain that Paula was sent by her boss to try to meet potential clients, but she's so shy she's not going to meet anyone without some serious help. I also make a point of letting Peggy know that Paula's firm isn't a member, so there may be an Alliance membership opportunity. Peggy points out another man that I should meet, and then follows me over to Paula. After making the introductions, I excuse myself from the conversation to go and meet him.

By the end of the evening, I've gathered the cards of five people who have agreed to get together with me, four who qualify as my potential geese and granny geese. The fifth, a gentleman by the name of Marv Fenster, is the executive director of Portland Home Care, an in-home nursing agency. He doesn't qualify as an egg, goose, or granny goose for me. In fact, nothing about him is of any particular interest to me. But I remembered that in-home nursing providers would be good for Nadia and Anton, so his card went into the pocket with the other keepers.

As the evening winds down and the crowd thins, I'm approached by Peggy. "Tyler, I have to go, but I wanted to tell you it was such a pleasure having you come and visit us."

"The pleasure was all mine, Peggy. I have to get going too. May I walk you out?"

"Sure. So, did you have a good time?" she asks as we make our way to the door.

"I had a wonderful time. You introduced me to some great people!"

We step out the door into the warm evening air and stop on the sidewalk. "Well, just so you know," she replies, "they came back to me and said the same thing about you. And that girl you introduced me to, we arranged to meet with her boss. Thank you so much for doing that! She told me you were the only person who even spoke to her."

"Yeah, she seemed like she was a little out of her element. I just tried to make her feel included."

"Well, that was very kind of you. You really know how to work a room."

"It was my pleasure."

"You're welcome to come to another event before making a decision to join the Alliance. Next Tuesday is a morning event called Shop Talk. It's an early morning mixer held monthly at the location of one of our members. Would you like to join us?"

"I'd love to!"

"Great. I'll e-mail you with all the details. Have a nice evening."

"You too, Peggy. Thanks again."

After we shake hands, I start up Jefferson Street toward the MAX station. Although past seven, the late July sun still hangs bright just above the West hills of Portland, bathing the neighborhood in gentle gold. Symbolic it seems of a very bright future made possible by this new way of doing business.

On the streetcar ride back to the Pearl District I take the opportunity to visit the websites of those whose cards I'd collected at the mixer. I'm amazed at how simple it was to connect with such high quality individuals in industries that fit so well with my Slarrefer business. I can't wait to show Oscar the results of my first networking event. Just as I finish my research, the streetcar makes its Tenth Avenue stop, right next to Powell's.

THIRTEEN

Following Up

The comforting aroma of books greets me as I enter the cavernous bookstore on the Southwest end of the Pearl district. If I had to assign a smell to a highly advanced civilization, it would be this smell.

Taking up the entire city block between NW Tenth and Eleventh Avenues and between W. Burnside and NW Couch Streets, Powell's City of Books is a maze of aisles lined with crowded bookshelves housed in rooms each identified by a color. In spite of its enormous size, containing over a million volumes made up of every kind of literature, there's still something cozy about the iconic Portland landmark. On more than one cold rainy day, I've found myself lost here in a remote corner, snuggled up to a warm book.

From the entrance at Tenth and Burnside, I make my way through the Green Room, past an information desk, and into a hallway displaying several carousels of greeting cards. As if it had been waiting for me, the right card catches my eye straight away. The cover displays an image of two hands embracing each other in greeting. The message on the inside reads, "It was nice to meet you." I grab all of them, about a dozen, and head back into the Green Room to the five-deep line at the register to pay for the cards and a book of stamps.

After being rung up by a purple-haired woman with matching thick, purple, horn-rimmed glasses and a demeanor so serious she seems more suited to military security than a bookstore sales clerk, I head up the walkway into the Blue Room, which leads me into the Gold Room. It's impossible to walk through the store without being slowed down in amazement at the tens of thousands of volumes of fiction. Walking past the science fiction section in the Gold Room, I surrender my attention to the bizarre cover of the *Small Assassin* by Ray Bradbury, which nearly causes me to bump into another store patron.

The aroma of espresso snaps me out of distraction. As I continue on, the book-shelves seem to part, revealing the opening to the coffee shop nestled in the Southwest corner of the building.

A sign above the entrance reads

WORLD CUP COFFEE
Browsing Limit 5 Books

The coffee shop is packed. I strain to spot an empty table. To my relief, I glimpse Oscar seated at a table by himself in the middle of the room, buried nose deep in a book, flanked by a cup of coffee and a scone. Without even looking up from the book, he motions for me to join him.

"So how'd your mixer go?" he asks without raising his eyes off the book as I lay my notepad and the sack of cards on the table.

"It was fantastic! I met a ton of people and have five hang outs to schedule!"

"Sounds like you have some follow up to do."

"I sure do."

He lays the book down, moves his glasses to the top of his head, rubs his eyes, and then raises his fists over his shoulders with a stretch. Curious, I reach over and turn the book around to read the title, *The Universe in a Nutshell*, by Stephen Hawking.

"Looks like you've been here awhile."

"All afternoon," Oscar groans. "And I never got past the Red Room! This is quite an establishment."

"They claim to be the largest independent new and used bookstore in the world."

"I can certainly believe it. So, let's see the business cards you collected," he says, perching his glasses back on his nose. I lay the five business cards on the table and give him a moment to look them over. "Very nice. This could be the start of a beautiful network," he says with a wink. "Let's get busy. Did you get the greeting cards?"

"Right here." I open the small paper sack containing the cards and hand him one.

He looks it over, then peers over his glasses and waves the card at me. "In these cards, you're going to write a sincere message of appreciation to each of these people for having met them, along with an invitation to get together to learn more about each other. You want to make the message about them, not about you. It should express your desire to get to know them better, including something about them that particu-larly interests you, the invitation to get together and a phone number where they can reach you. Avoid the temptation to put anything self promotional in the note, other-wise you'll get very little response."

He picks up his scone and takes a bite while wiggling an index finger at the cards on the table before me, telling me to get busy, then goes back to his book. After a moment of thought, I remove the pen from my pocket and compose a message to the estate planning attorney.

I finish writing the card and hand it to Oscar for his inspection.

He glances at it and hands it back.

"Perfect. Short and simple. Get this into the mail tonight. The sooner she receives it, the better. Tomorrow morning, give her a call to set an appointment to get together. If you're unable to reach her directly, leave a message reminding her of your conversation and that you're calling to set a time to get together.

You're going to follow these steps with each of those whom you met at the mixer this evening. In the case of those who you reach directly, your note should be received two or three days after your phone call. In any case, they'll have received it by the time you do meet. That'll make you a far more interesting person to get to know because you've shown a genuine interest in them."

"This is great, Oscar. If I met someone at a networking event and they followed up with me like this, I'd be all over the idea of getting together with them."

"As will about nine out of ten people with whom you follow up with in this manner. Now I'm going to share something with you that may sound a little like," he pauses and looks to the ceiling trying to find the right words, "like flakey pseudo-science. However, trust what I am about to tell you and allow the results to speak for themselves."

"I trust you, Oscar."

"Good. Any time you send a card to someone, you transmit your relational energy."

"What does that mean?"

"It means that, regardless of what you write in the card, your true intentions will be received on an unconscious level."

"I still don't understand."

"Let me put it this way. If your note says you want to get together to learn more about the recipient and their business, but your true intention is to just get to their network or to sell them your wares, that intention will be received unconsciously. The recipient may not perceive it consciously, but there'll be something about you that they can't quite put their finger on that'll prevent them from trusting you completely."

"But I do sincerely want to meet her to learn about her and her law practice. She could be a tremendous resource for my Slarrefer clients and the others I network with."

"I know you do. Just keep what I've said in the back of your mind. It'll serve you well into the future as you go forth to build your network. As long as you write these cards from your heart, you'll be fine."

"You're right. It does sound like soft science," I respond. "And if it had been any-one else telling me about something called relational energy, I'd probably be skeptical. But radio waves and photosynthesis and gravity are phenomena that have never been explained to my satisfaction, but I accept them as real because I've seen the evidence. So I don't have any problem with the idea of relational energy, but it does sound weird."

Oscar points at his watch to indicate that it's getting late, "Better finish writing the rest of those cards if want to get them into the mail tonight," he goads, then goes back to reading his book.

After several minutes, I finish writing all but one of the cards. Not sure how to ap-proach Marv, the director of the in-home nursing agency, I turn to Oscar. "Hey, Oscar, how do I handle this one, the guy who runs the in-home nursing outfit? He's not a potential egg—at least I don't think he is. And he's not a goose or a granny goose. But he's definitely a potential goose for the folks at the medical supply shop. Do I hang out with him or just make an introduction?"

He stops reading and peers over his glasses at me. "What do you know of this person?"

"Other than what's on his card, I don't know anything."

"Then why would you make an introduction?"

"Because he runs an in-home nursing outfit, which could be an ideal referral source for Nadia and Anton."

"If you saw a bus bench with an advertisement painted on it for an in-home health care agency, would you write down that information and pass it along to these people because it might be a good referral source?"

"Well, no."

"Why not?"

"Because I don't know who I'd be referring to them. Its just information on a bus bench."

"And what you have there is just information on a card."

"But I met the guy."

"So what did you learn during that handshake that convinced you he would be a valuable resource for the medical supply shop owners?"

"Well, I mentioned that I knew a couple that owned a medical supply business that is looking for in-home health care agencies to network with. He said he'd love to meet them. And he's in a profession that Nadia and Anton thought might be a likely source of referrals for them. But other than that, I don't really know anything. "

"Anytime you give a referral or make an introduction, your reputation and the relationship you have with those you're introducing are on the line. Best to know who it is you're referring. I'd certainly take the time to get to know this individual and his business before making an introduction."

"So you're saying I should hang out with him as well?"

"Absolutely. It's all part of tending the garden."

With a sigh, I begin writing the last card inviting Marv to meet for coffee. I'm beginning to feel overwhelmed at the number of meetings I've now committed myself to. After completing the note, I stuff, address, and stamp each of the envelopes and then check the time: 8:15 pm. Still plenty of time to stop at the post office on the way home before the day's last pickup at ten.

"Done," I announce.

Oscar lifts his head from his book. "Good job. Now was that all that difficult?"

"No, it was pretty easy. But it was one more thing to do."

"One more thing that, if practiced consistently, will create extraordinary results. Remember, effective follow-up is easy, but it's a rare individual who actually implements it. Can you repeat the steps for me?"

"Yeah, I think so. First, when I meet someone at an event, I invite her to hang out. Second, I get her card and make sure there's a physical mailing address. Third, I immediately send her a heartfelt card inviting her to get together with me. I make the card about her, not about me. Fourth, I call her the next day to schedule a time to get together as we discussed."

"Excellent!" Oscar exclaims.

"And if I get a voicemail, I leave a message. I shouldn't worry if she doesn't return the call right away, because people are just busy. Most of them will return my call when they get the greeting card."

"You're a fast learner, kid. I give you an A for this lesson. Make these steps a habit, and you'll have people clamoring to hang out with you."

"Thanks. It's easy when you have such a great teacher."

"It's what I do," he says with a shrug. "Now, schmoozing at a chamber mixer is just one way to find prospective networking partners. There are other organized opportunities for networking that you should be aware of. In our next lesson we'll focus on exploring business organizations whose memberships might specifically include your geese and your granny geese, such as industry associations.

"Hope it's as fun and interesting as going to the chamber mixer turned out to be."

"At least as much fun and probably even more interesting."

"You said we'd cover social media at some point too," I remind him.

"I think we can squeeze that in. How about deciding when we're going to get together next?"

I pull out my phone and scroll to the calendar. "Tomorrow I've got two hang outs, the first at eleven and the other at one. Then I have to be in the office for a meeting at three thirty. My first meeting is just a few blocks from here. This place opens at nine in the morning. How about we meet back here a little after that?"

"Works for me. In the meantime, you better get those into the mail," he says, pointing to the stack of cards, "and then get home to get your clothes in the wash before that mocha stain sets."

"What mocha stain?" I ask, looking down at the front of my shirt. As the words leave my mouth, I'm jolted out of my chair by a loud SPLORSH and the shock of an ice-cold liquid running down my back.

"Oh my gosh! Oh my gosh! I'm so sorry."

I jump out of my chair and turn to see the panicked young woman who has just tripped and spilled what I can now safely guess was an iced mocha down my back. The barista runs over from behind the counter with a handful of napkins, but not before I feel the cold, slightly sticky drink making its way down the inside of my pants and down the back of my leg.

After a couple of minutes listening to profuse apologies, I've managed to soak up most of it with the help of the barista and the woman. I reassure the young lady that it was just an accident, and that I'll be fine, but I am anxious to get home and out of these clothes. I pick up my notepad, phone, and the greeting cards off the table. Of course, Oscar is nowhere to be seen. Amid the uncomfortable stares of other customers, I make my way out of the bookstore and to my car as quickly as I can.

Once in the car it only takes me ten minutes to make it home, even with the stop at the post office box. Remembering my promise to Oscar, I retrieve the teapot from the back seat and rush upstairs to change out of my sticky, mocha soaked clothes.

FOLLOW UP

1. After event follow up with a handwritten note. Get it into the mail the same day if possible.

BUY GREETING CARDS

2. Call the next day to set appointment. Remember, step one is setting the expectation for my call by asking the person at the event if they would be open to getting together to learn more about each others' business.

Once I invite someone to hang out, get their card. Make sure there's a physical mailing address. Immediately follow up with a heart-felt card. Make the card about them, not about me. Call the next day to schedule a time to get together (as we discussed).

If get a voicemail, leave a message. Don't worry if they don't return the call right away. Most will return my call when they get the card.

Send an e-mail or call again if I don't hear back in about 5 days.

FOURTEEN

It's Just a Teapot

"Hey, Baxter," I call to the black-and-white alley cat who adopted me a couple of years before Karen and I were married. Baxter's been a steady, though emotionally distant, companion for the last few years. He offers affection sparingly, usually when he thinks he can get a tummy rub out of it, and never misses an opportunity to remind me that he's in power. If I were to research what species of cat he is, I imagine it would be something like *Felis selfimporticus*.

I've just returned from the laundry room to find him engrossed in a close examination of the teapot, which I left on the kitchen counter. Giving into my own curiosity, I decide to join him and take a closer look.

"I'm home!" Karen shouts over the sound of the front door closing behind her. She steps into the kitchen to find me in a pair of shorts, slippers, and a tank top examining the inside of the teapot with a penlight while Baxter sits on the counter keeping a close watch.

"Hey, babe," I reply without looking up.

"What are you two doing?"

"Just checking out the teapot. Every time I touch this I feel the sensation of electricity, but otherwise I can't find anything remarkable about it. How the hell does he fit in here?"

Karen places her purse on the counter as I continue to peer inside. "Is this *the* teapot?" she asks anxiously.

"Yeah." I pick it up, offering it to her to hold. "Here, touch it."

Cautiously, she takes it from my hands, slowly shakes it, looks inside, and places it back on the counter. "It's just an old teapot."

"Don't you feel it?"

"Feel what?"

"Like . . . electricity. Don't you feel that charge coming off it?"

She gives me a very worried look. "I'm sorry, sweetie. I don't feel anything. It's just a teapot, and an ugly one at that."

"Let me show you something." I pick my briefcase up off the floor and pull out the notepad. "Do you see these notes?" I ask as I show her the pages that Oscar drew his examples on the other day.

"Yes."

"Karen, he wrote this. These are the notes Oscar wrote while we were talking."

"He has very nice penmanship," she answers with a not so subtle hint of sarcasm.

I try to hide my anger at her patronizing response. She has every right to be concerned about me. I have to remind myself that giving her further cause to suspect that I'm coming unglued, on top of our financial pressures, is not a burden I want to place on the person I love more than anything.

Confused and hurt, I return the notepad back to the briefcase and gather up the teapot with an angry sigh. Not sure where I should put it, I glance back to ask Karen. Her anguish-filled expression tells me I've just crossed over the line, convincing her that there's something seriously wrong with me. Baxter leaps off the counter and cowers under the coffee table, as if he can tell trouble's brewing. I drop the briefcase, put the teapot back on the counter, step toward her, and hold her face in my hands. "Baby, please. I promise you I'm not losing my mind. I know it's hard to believe any of this, but he's real."

She's trembling, which is scaring the hell out of me. I look back at the teapot. "Oscar, you gotta help me out here. Just show her you're real. Please!"

Nothing happens. I look back at Karen. The horrified expression on her face tells me that trying to call Oscar from the teapot only made things a lot worse. I open my mouth to say something to reassure her, but nothing comes out. She bursts into tears, grabs her purse, and runs into the bedroom.

"Wait, sweetie!"

The apartment shakes from the bedroom door slamming behind her. I collapse onto the sofa and place my face in my hands. This is the moment I was trying to avoid. I lift my head up, lean back, stare at the ceiling with a sigh, and then turn to look at the teapot. "Thanks a lot, pal. Looks like I'll be sleeping here on the couch tonight."

A lump of fur lands on my lap. The couch is Baxter's favorite nightspot. With an annoyed meow, he lets me know he's not all pleased about the idea of sharing.

FIFTEEN

Where to Network

I'm at the counter of the coffee shop in Powell's Books waiting for my order. It's just after nine o'clock on Friday morning. The place is already crowded with people having coffee meetings, working on their laptops, and thumbing through books.

After a sleepless night of tossing and turning on the couch, I have a sort of hangover. Not a too-much-alcohol-guts-churning hangover, but a not-enough-sleep, head-in-a-fog kind of hangover, the kind where you're sort of okay as long as you don't have to concentrate on anything too hard.

"House blend with four shots?" the barista calls out. I take the cup of supercharged coffee and stagger over to Oscar. He's at the same table we sat at last night, this time with two others: a gray-haired sixtyish woman reading something with the words *Feminist Psychology* on the cover and a young man studying on a laptop. I toss my notebook on the table, and with an involuntary groan, plop down in the empty seat next to him.

"What happened to you?"

In no hurry to start the conversation, I sip my coffee before responding. My neck feels like a garage door spring, and the angry knot in my upper back stabs at me with electric daggers. "I didn't get much sleep," I answer, craning my neck back and forth in search of some relief. "Why, do I look that bad?"

"Other than the half-closed bloodshot eyes, turned-out collar, shirt buttons all off by one hole, and cat fur all over your trousers, not at all," he replies sarcastically. "You spend the night under a bridge or something?"

"Or something."

"Talk to me."

I rest my elbows on the table and grind the heels of my palms into my eye sockets in an attempt to rub away the previous eight hours of tossing and turning. "I got into it with Karen last night. She locked me out of the bedroom again, so I spent the night on the couch." I moan. "Feels like the couch spent the night on me."

"I don't understand why you keep picking fights with that poor girl," he says non-chalantly, holding a saucer in one hand and bringing a cup of coffee to his lips with the other.

"You're the reason she's mad at me," I snap as he innocently takes a sip.

With a loud clank, he puts the saucer and cup on the table. "How am I responsible for your wife being mad at you? I've never even met your wife."

"And that's the problem. She's not sure if I'm on drugs or if I've completely lost my mind. Either way, I'm skating on very thin ice, thanks to you."

"Thanks to me?" he protests.

"I can't be keeping secrets from her, Oscar. I had to tell her about you living in the teapot and how you've been traveling through time since ancient Babylon."

The woman across the table lifts her head from her book and looks at us with a raised eyebrow.

"You *had* to tell her?" he raises his voice. "There's a difference between being open with your wife and running off at the mouth about my personal life." He grows more animated, waving his arms with exaggerated gestures. "First you treat my home like an empty soda can. Next, you're spreading gossip about my age and where I live, and now you have the nerve to suggest that I'm the cause of your marital woes?" He crosses his arms, turns his head away, and lets out an indignant "Harrumph."

I can't tell if he's playing with me again or if he's really upset, and I don't care. "This is serious, Oscar. I brought the teapot home just like I promised. When I showed it to her, she started freaking out, so I called for you to show yourself. Where were you?"

He picks up his coffee, takes another drink, and casually replies, "I didn't hear you. I might've been in the shower."

"In the sh—" Exasperated, I stop myself mid-sentence. It's obvious I'm not going to get a straight answer. Besides, I'd just get distracted wondering if the teapot does have a shower, and, if so, what kind of self-contained plumbing he's got in there.

"You know Oscar, none of this hanging out for a living shit means anything if I lose the most important person in my life!" I shout, barely noticing the people at the other tables turning toward us to see what the commotion is. The woman across the table slams her book shut and quickly leaves.

Oscar glances around the room and lowers his voice. "Get a grip, kid. Look, you and your wife'll be fine," he reassures me. "I promise she'll understand the mysteries of the teapot before she files for a divorce."

Now the young man is looking at us with an intrigued expression.

"Before she files for a divorce? Holy smokes, how far out of hand does this situation have to get before you help me prove to her she doesn't need to have an intervention?"

He gives me a sort of nervous, guilty look, and then turns his eyes to the ceiling.

"My wife is planning an intervention?"

"The poor girl's worried about you. You have been acting kind of squirrelly, you know. Put yourself in her shoes. If she started talking to teapots, what would you do?"

"Aaaarrrgghh," I groan, returning my face to the palm of my hands.

"Listen, in a couple of months, when my assignment with you is complete, everything will make sense to her. In the meantime, you gotta pull yourself together, kid. We got work to do."

"In a couple of months! Oh, Oscar, what're you doing to me?" I cry into my hands.

He places his hand on my shoulder. "Look, I understand you're in an awkward situation—"

"An awkward situation, he says." I raise my voice in response to his understatement.

With indignation, Oscar again crosses his arms. "We can skip today's lesson if you're not up to it."

I take a deep breath and try to compose myself. "No, no, I'm with you. The coffee just needs to kick in." I throw back a large gulp. "Look, I'm sorry I went off on you. I know you're only here to help. In fact, seems like you're the only one in my life that isn't out to fire me, collect from me, sue me, or have me committed."

"Don't worry about it. Tell you what, I'll see what I can do to make things right with your bride. But right now, we need to resume our lessons, so listen up," he demands, knocking three times on the table to get my attention. "I don't want to have to repeat myself because you're off in la-la-land when you should be listening."

"I'm listening," I growl.

"Good," he answers, acting oblivious to my aggravated state.

~Industry Associations~

"Yesterday we covered how to find, and then directly experience, a chamber of commerce networking event. Today we're going to add industry-specific organizations, such as trade and professional associations to the discussion.

"Most industry and trade associations offer an affiliate membership to those who don't specifically work or practice within that industry, but who may be in a position of serving that industry. For example, a real estate association may have landscapers, plumbers, or exterminators as members, even though they themselves are not part of the real estate profession."

"Because they can help prepare a property for a sale, there's an affiliation?" I interject.

"Exactly. Remember a couple of days ago when you determined that a potential granny goose for you might be a bar association?"

"Yeah, I remember," I answer as I clumsily flip back through my notepad to the pages I wrote those notes on.

"As I recall, the reason you felt a bar association might be a granny goose is because they would have a network of your potential geese, estate planning attorneys."

"Right. And I came to that conclusion because estate planning attorneys would, by nature of their business, likely have a network of individuals and couples between the ages of fifty and seventy who live in the greater Portland/Vancouver metropolitan area, have grown children, are financially well off, are retired or close to retirement, and are looking for a way to preserve a financial legacy for their heirs," I answer, reading from my notes.

"So let's see what local bar associations are in the area and what kind of memberships they may have available for you non-attorney types. Pull out your magic gizmo and let's see what we can find out about the local bar association."

~Show Up in Contribution~

I open my laptop and google *Portland bar association*. We both watch as the search returns a few county bar associations. I click the first one, and we both read the web page. "There! Right there," Oscar exclaims, pointing at the link on the side of the website that says *Membership*. I click the link, opening a drop-down menu. One of the options says *Join/Renew*. It leads to a membership form offering several different membership options. "There ya go," he says, pointing at the screen and then leaning back confidently with an "I told you so" expression.

Sure enough, one of the options reads: *Affiliate Member: Any member of the general public who does not fit the criteria of any other membership category—$150*

"Oscar, this is amazing. I can join a bar association!"

"Of course you can."

"Yeah, but . . . well I just thought you had to be a lawyer or at least work in the legal profession on some level to get in there."

"You think too much, kid. Now, before you go gettin' yourself in a tizzy, let's talk about how you're going to contribute to the association."

"What do you mean how I'm going to contribute? I don't even know how I'd swing the $150 they want for membership dues."

"I'm not talking about the membership fee."

I lay my pen down and let Oscar finish.

"Time to reiterate a point that I made earlier, and that is what you give away you get back in spades. Remember the fundamental law of hanging for a living, that it's only possible to hang out for a living if one does so in service to others?"

"Yeah."

"That applies to organizations as well as individuals. You've logically concluded that the bar association would have a network of people that you desire to build a professional relationship with: estate planning attorneys, who might have clients that fit the description of your ideal client.

"For you to successfully build fruitful relationships within the association, you must come from a place of contribution rather than one of personal gain."

"So how do I contribute?"

"With your knowledge and with your attitude. You bring knowledge that'll be helpful to attorneys. That, combined with an attitude of helpfulness, will make you an invaluable member of the organization."

"Oscar, I'm a struggling Yellow Page advertising sales associate who's just getting his feet wet in the financial services industry. What knowledge or experience do I have that would be helpful to people who have been through years of law school and have passed the bar exam? Seems I'd be pretty far out of my league."

"It's not about the knowledge and experience you have. It's about the knowledge and experience you have access to that you can bring to the association."

"You lost me."

"Okay," he says tapping his chin while looking up to think of an appropriate example. "Let's say you were to offer a lunch-and-learn program. You could prepare a forty-five minute talk about financial tips and strategies that would be beneficial to the clients of estate planning attorneys. You'd provide your audience with knowledge that enables them to add value to their clients. You give valuable information away that your audience would be happy to pay for in any other circumstance. You might even consult with the association about what is required to qualify such a presentation for Continuing Education Credit. Do this without any expectation of your audience having to use your company. In other words, you're not there to sell them anything. But, by providing high value, an amazing thing will happen at the conclusion of such a presentation."

"What?" I ask with anticipation.

"Several of those in attendance will line up anxiously to talk to you and request your card."

"This is an incredible idea, Oscar, but I'm not ready to do a lunch-and-learn or offer continuing education to attorneys. I'm still learning the Slarrefer program. What knowledge and experience can I possibly give them?"

"You're overcomplicating it. Again, it's not about the knowledge and experience you have. It's about giving value to your audience. Simply have a more senior representative who does have the knowledge and experience do the program with you. The way you've described the company's network marketing structure, there must be an upline person with some level of experience and success who would be willing to help you."

"Of course! My regional manager would flip if I asked him to do that with me," I respond while slapping my forehead at the ridiculously obvious answer. "I think I'm getting it. I simply use my resources to bring value to the attorneys."

"You *are* getting it," he says with a reassuring smile. "It's your attitude of service that will make you a valuable person to know, which is why people will want to have a relationship with you. And, over time, you'll gain the experience. Meanwhile, you'll become known as a valuable resource and as a connector. That'll build trust and credibility. There are those in your field with years of experience who have never built trust or credibility. Far better to be the former rather than the latter."

"So it's better to be a neophyte gardener than an experienced hunter?"

"Well said, kid," Oscar says.

"Another way to contribute would be to serve on a committee. Business organizations like the bar association or the chamber of commerce all have committees which serve the members, the business community, or the community at large. Such committees are usually made up of volunteer members who have business expertise or interests that fit particularly well with the mission of that particular committee. Serving on such a committee would allow you to contribute and might also provide you with unique relational and business opportunities.

"So let's get started. Find the name and number of the membership director," he says, leaning back and resting his coffee cup on his belly.

After scrolling around the site for several moments, I discover a link that says *Staff.* One of the listings says *Office & Membership Administrator—Moira Repeeketag.*

"I think I found something," I announce, showing the screen to Oscar.

"Perfect, now call this Moira and explain that you have an interest in participating in the association, but before you make a decision, you want to make sure you can actually contribute. Ask if she would do you the honor of allowing you to buy her lunch so that you can pick her brain about some ideas you have about that."

"That's great! Who wouldn't want get a call like that?"

"Easy, boy. This isn't a guaranteed hole-in-one. I think you'll find that the membership staff of most business organizations like this will accept that offer, but it really depends upon how much contact this person is allowed to have with the outside world. The membership process for this bar association appears to take place entirely online, which may be a clue that this person either can't or won't take you up on your offer. You won't know until you make the call."

He sets his coffee cup on the table and gives me a "What are you waiting for?" look. I call the number. A voice answers after two rings.

"This is Moira."

"Hi, Moira, my name is Tyler Cirella. Are you the person I would talk to about an affiliate membership in the association?"

"Yes, Tyler. Did you have a question?" she asks in a tone that sounds like I've interrupted something important.

"I'm interested in learning more about an affiliate membership. You see, I'm not an attorney, but I believe my company's financial services would be something estate planning attorneys would—"

"What is your company, Tyler?" she interrupts.

"We're called Slarrefer Mutual."

"I can't say I'm familiar with you."

"Well, I'm calling because it seems like an affiliate membership would be worth looking into. I want to make sure I can make a positive contribution before I make that decision. Would you be open to letting me buy you lunch so I can share some ideas with you, and you can tell me more about the association?"

"I don't really have time for outside lunches, Tyler. If you'd like to come by the office, though, I'd be happy to meet with you."

"Umm . . . sure, that would be fine."

"I can see you at ten on Tuesday morning."

"Can you hold on while I check my calendar?"

"Certainly," she replies.

I check my calendar and find that I've scheduled three hang outs before that days' afternoon phone-a-thon.

"I'm pretty slammed on Tuesday. How's Wednesday around two o'clock?"

"Staff meeting. How about Thursday at ten?"

"Ten thirty would be better."

"Ten thirty it is. I look forward to meeting you next Thursday, Tyler."

"See you then, Moira. Have a great weekend!"

I lay my phone on the table and turn to Oscar. "Man, that one's all business. She shut me down on the lunch idea pretty quickly, but agreed to meet me at the association next Thursday."

"Good enough. Now, let's discuss how to effectively participate in an association."

"Okay."

~Relational Capital~

"An entity like an association," he explains, "only becomes a granny goose when it leads you to your potential geese. An association usually has at least two or three people with the kind of specific relational capital required to introduce you to the geese you seek. Who do you think they might be?"

"Relational capital?"

"They know lots of people," he clarifies.

"Well, this Moira gal, because she's in charge of membership. Seems she'd have to have met everyone at some point."

"Probably. You'll notice that she also holds the position of office administrator, which means she's effectively the gatekeeper. That's what makes her likely to know everyone. Depending upon the organization, though, membership and administrative duties may be performed by different people. Someone whose only function is membership may very well be able to connect you to your geese. But then again, if that person's only job is processing electronic applications, they may never actually build relationships with anyone. Therefore, when exploring an association, it can't hurt to put the name of the person in charge of membership high on the list of people to get to know. Once you reach out to them in the manner you just did with this Moira, you'll discover how connected they actually are. In just about every case, though, they'll at least be able to introduce you to those who are well connected."

"Is that why you suggested I buy her lunch?"

"I suggested lunch because it's an environment that tends to foster a productive conversation about how to effectively participate in the association. However, a good meal does have a way of making people more willing to make introductions," he replies with a wink. "So, who else within such an organization might know everyone?"

"The president, or whomever the head cheese is?"

"Good answer. The president should go on that same list of people to get to know. However, individuals in a role of leadership of an association are often operating a business or practice in addition to serving the association. That compound burden of responsibility can often prevent them from engaging you with a level of attention required to develop any kind of meaningful relationship. Let's shoot for some lower hanging fruit."

I rack my brain trying to think of whom else within an association might be well connected and accessible, but come up empty. "I'm stuck."

"There are usually at least two individuals within an association who are more likely than others to have the relational capital you seek. There's the gatekeeper, who's usually a secretary for the president or whomever it is that handles the administrative business, like this Moira gal."

"Oh, yeah," I remark as I write my notes.

"And the immediate past president."

"Immediate past president?"

"Yes. Unless this organization is brand new, there had to have been someone who preceded the current president."

"So what makes them any better than the current president?"

"Think about it. As the president, or whatever the title may be, that person had to have huge relational capital within the organization. They don't lose that once their term expires. So the immediate past president retains the relational capital that came with the position, but is no longer burdened with the responsibility of holding that position."

"Wow, Oscar, I never would have thought of that! So the immediate past president would be someone I'd want to get to know."

"In most cases. And the best way to meet such a person would be to get introduced to them. So who might be able to introduce you to the immediate past president of an association?"

"Well, we just said the membership director or the gatekeeper or someone else within the organization."

"Or?" Oscar asks with a dramatic pause as he lifts his coffee cup, as if I'm supposed to finish his thought.

"Or what?"

"Who else might introduce you to the immediate past president, or the president, or to anyone else whom you might seek to develop a relationship with?"

"I don't know. Who? Who?" I ask anxiously.

He leaves me hanging as he sips his coffee, in no rush to provide me with an answer. I stare at him expectantly, and after several moments, he answers. "How about those you hang out with?"

"How would someone I happen to be hanging out with know the past president of an association?"

"They may not. You're missing the point. When you're hanging out with someone and the questions 'How can I help you?' or 'Who can I introduce you to?' come up, you might want to give them the name of someone you seek to be introduced to, like the past president of an association. You never know who their next door neighbor, sister-in-law, church acquaintance, best friend from high school, or fellow softball team member may be."

"Of course, especially in a close-knit town like Portland where there's only like two degrees of separation between everyone," I reply, shaking my head for not coming up with the obvious answer myself.

"Don't sweat it," Oscar replies, staring into his now empty coffee cup. "Like we discussed the other day, when you determined that the bar association might be a potential granny goose, you need to find a whom. The name of the organization just helps you identify the species of goose, but it's actually the individuals within the organization that do the honking," he says playfully while wagging his eyebrows. I smile back, too exhausted to really appreciate the pun. "This completes our lesson about business organizations. Any questions before we move on?"

"No, I think I'm good," I groggily reply, followed by a wide yawn.

"Very well. Before we continue, I could use a refill," he says tilting his empty coffee cup and looking inside it. "And you sure look like you could use another cup of that motor oil you've been drinking."

"I sure could."

"I'll get it," Oscar announces over the high-pitched grating sound his chair makes as he pushes it back from the table. "That was an Americano with four shots, right?"

"Just make it six straight espresso shots," I mumble before dropping my head on the notepad with a thud.

Associations

Join for the purpose of contributing

Call membership director to find out about
an affiliate membership. Offer to buy lunch to
discuss how I might be able to contribute, i.e.
    - Lunch and learn.
    - Serve on a committee.

Seek out those who have relational capital.
- Membership director?
- Office administrator?
- President?
- Immediate past-president?

Business development (referral) groups
- Get introduced to a referral group with
high membership standards.
- Visit a meeting to observe (notice how they
make me feel).
- Hang out with some of the members.

Service Clubs

Join to support the cause, allow the
networking to happen.

Rember to ask those I hang out with for
introductions to the people I want to meet.

SIXTEEN

Where Else to Network

"Hey, Van Winkle, here's your joy juice," I hear Oscar say over the sound of a ceramic coffee cup landing gently on the table next to my head. I crack open an eye and see his sideways-cocked head come into view as he bends down to look back at me. "Anyone in there?"

"Yeah," I reply as I lift my head. "Someone's in here . . . at least part of someone. I think." I blink my eyes to get some focus. "Thanks."

"For a minute there I thought I was going to have to give it to you in an IV."

I smirk at the comment, and then take as big a gulp as I can without scalding my mouth. "Okay, I'm back with you," I announce, flipping to a fresh sheet of paper.

Oscar raises an eyebrow, indicating that he's not at all convinced that I am.

~Business Development Groups~

"All right then," he continues, "I want you to be aware of a couple of other types of organizations through which you might expand your network. The first are business development groups, which might also be called referral groups. These are groups of people who get together specifically for the purpose of referring business to, or collaborating with, each other. Some groups operate independently and others exist as chapters of an established national or international referral organization."

"There are national and international referral organizations?"

"Of course."

"How come I've never heard of them?"

"Probably because you've never been invited. Membership within such groups, at least the good ones, is usually by invitation."

"How do they work?"

"Typically such a group meets weekly and has a strict structure to its gatherings to ensure that the event begins and ends on time and fulfills a specific agenda. A quality group will be made up of professionals, each one representing a particular industry or area of expertise. Some only allow one person per profession, the idea being to prevent competition and confusion within the group. Others have no such restriction, but instead require that the members participate in the spirit of collaboration."

"And they all refer business to me?"

"Not by a long shot. Some in the group will be better equipped to refer business to you than others. However, embracing such a group as a vehicle for expanding your network, rather than as a source of clients, would be far more effective and infinitely more valuable. Remember, it's a lot easier for people to give and receive introductions to geese and granny geese than it is to refer potential clients."

"Being part of a group of people who understand the granny goose formula would be amazing."

"Indeed it would."

"So how do I find such a group?"

"The method you used to find the business alliance and the bar association would be one way. However, being invited to such a group by a trusted member of your network would be preferable. Add *an introduction to a referral group with high standards* to your list of ways others can help you."

I flip to a page in my notes I've set aside just for ideas about how others can help me.

"Now, it's important that you join the right group. Just as you want to prevent weeds from invading your garden, you want to avoid planting your roots in a garden of weeds."

"What do you mean?"

"Not all business development groups are created equal, not even those that belong to the same parent organization. Therefore, I recommend taking your time to find the right group."

"So how will I know if I've found the right group?"

"The same way you determine whether or not someone is the kind of person you want in your network. Just as you'll encounter individuals who don't display the integrity, relational capital, or spirit of service required to be part of your network, you will encounter many groups that don't embody the spirit of hanging out in service to others. A couple of visits to a business development group will inform you whether or not it's a good group by observing the standards by which they operate."

"So what standards should I be looking for?"

"One standard would be the group's established membership guidelines. If I were you, I wouldn't join a group that would allow me in without first doing some due diligence. The kind of group you want to be part of would be reluctant to allow you to join simply because you're not yet established in your business, and that is a very good thing. Be wary of a referral group that allows you in simply because there is no one else representing your field."

"That sort of make sense, but it puts me in a kind of catch-22. Sounds like you're saying the only referral group that would good enough for me is a group that wouldn't have me because I'm not good enough to join them."

"No, I'm saying that a reputable group will check you out thoroughly, ask for references, and have a few of their members hang out with you to get a sense of who you are. Strict membership guidelines aren't there to disqualify good people who would bring value to the group. They're there to eliminate those who won't."

"So I can tell if it's a good group by how hard they make it to join?"

"That's only one potential indicator," Oscar answers. "I'd suggest visiting one of their gatherings so that you can actually witness the standards they operate by. Notice whether the meeting begins and ends at the time advertised. That reflects the respect they have for their members' time.

"Take note of who's in the group. Does the group require that the members are *really* in business, or do they allow dabblers and hobbyists? A group that allows members who are just dabbling in a business is, in all likelihood, a patch of weeds. Therefore, you want to be part of a group that enforces a standard of membership.

"Hang out with some of the members. Allow them to get to know you while you get to know them."

He drinks his coffee slowly, allowing me to finish writing. With a nod I signal him to continue.

"And, most important, trust your gut. How does the group make you feel? If it's a good group, visitors are made to feel like the most important and welcome people in the room, even if they're not a fit for the group.

"Enjoy the process of finding a referral group. It's a lot like finding the right girl. You'll just know it when it happens," he says with a wink. "At this early stage, you're still in the process of becoming a master networker. It won't be long before you're not only good enough to join such a group, but you'll become the person people will be clamoring to have as part of their referral group. In the meantime, explore business development groups so that, when you're ready, you'll be able to make an informed choice about which group to join."

I complete my notes with a loud tap of my pencil and announce, "Got it. I'm glad you're not telling me to join a group like this right away. My plate's already pretty full."

"Pace yourself, kid, and you'll be fine."

~Service Groups~

"Next there are service groups or clubs. Service groups generally exist for the purpose of giving back through charitable activities. These groups are made up of people who unite not for the purpose of doing business, but to serve the community or to support a particular cause."

"You mean like a Rotary Club or the Kiwanis?"

"Or the Lions or Elks or Shriners, yes. Such groups are often made up of business people, though that's not usually a membership requirement. What is required is having the time, finances, and most important, the desire to contribute. You should never join such a group for the purpose of networking. Your reason for participating must be because you believe in the causes that the group stands for, and because you're committed to supporting the group in that mission. The beautiful thing, though, is that networking tends to occur between those within the group."

"Yeah, I can see how that would happen."

"Now, for the purpose of networking, social clubs fall into the same category as service groups. A vintage car club, for example, or even the Red Hat Society would also work."

"Oscar, something tells me I'd have a hard time getting into the Red Hats."

"Ha! It's just an example, kid. The idea is that these are environments where people socialize. A church or a gym could also fit the model, depending upon how socially active one is within that group."

"So I don't go there to find people to network with, I go there to participate, but by participating the networking just happens?" I answer, rephrasing Oscar's words to make sure I understand.

"Exactly! Think of it like fishing. You ever gone fishing?"

"Sure."

"Think very carefully before you answer my next question. Why did you go fishing? I mean, why did you really go?"

I ponder the question for a moment. "To get away, relax, to clear my head?" I answer in the form of a question, not sure what Oscar's looking for.

"But what about the fish? You didn't mention fish. Don't you have to catch fish?"

"Well, I didn't really go fishing for fish. I went to unwind in a relaxing environment. I'm not really much of a fisherman. I think catching fish is just sort of a bonus if it happens. A fresh-caught fish cooked over a camp fire can be pretty tasty if you can get past the gamey taste, but on at least a couple of occasions I just threw back what I caught."

"In other words, you didn't really go to fish. You went to get away and relax. You just called it fishing. Catching fish was secondary to the primary purpose of your trip, which was to relax."

"Yeah, it was more about passing the time and unwinding than catching fish."

"The difference between fishing at the lake and networking in a service or social group is simply what you call it. When you went fishing, you were really relaxing, but were happy to let some fishing happen. When you participate in a service group, you're there to serve, but some hanging out will happen."

"I get it. Be there for the right reason, and allow the rest to happen as a fringe benefit."

"You *have* got it! And I assure you, the rest will happen."

~Online Networking~

With a loud yawn, I raise my fists and stretch.

"You still with me?" Oscar asks.

"Yeah, I'm good. That espresso really helped."

"Good. Any questions?"

"Yeah. I know a lot has changed since your last assignment, Oscar, but today most networking happens online through social media. You haven't even mentioned it."

"Ah, yes, meeting people without meeting people."

"Oscar, that's the direction the world's going. I get how important meeting people in person is, but it seems like hanging out with people is analog behavior in a digital world. Remember the candlemaker?"

"So you're concerned that hanging out with people to develop strategic business relationships when you could just connect with people from the comfort of your digital device is analogous to lighting dark places with candles when there are light bulbs that can do so more efficiently?"

"I'm saying that I'm not sure how the hanging out formula will apply as the digital age evolves."

"It'll continue to apply in exactly the same way as it did one hundred, two hundred, or two thousand years ago. The quality of trust and rapport that physically hanging out creates cannot be achieved in a virtual world. Therefore, the candlemaker analogy doesn't apply because you can't accomplish the same thing from a digital device."

"Oscar, people are developing profitable relationships all over the world without ever meeting in person."

"True. But those people aren't hanging out. They're tapping away at keyboards and staring at computer screens. They may be generating profits, but they're missing out on the happiness and fulfillment of hanging out. My boy, if you confined yourself to such an environment, you'd shrivel up and die."

"So the formula can't be applied in the digital world?"

"I didn't say that. Digital technology, if applied properly, can be a very powerful tool for sowing the relational garden."

"How do I properly apply it?"

"By using it for the purpose of finding potential geese, granny geese, and networking partners. It's the same as finding the people you want to meet at a networking event. You go there to find them, but you don't hang out there with them. Cyberspace is not the environment to develop a relationship, at least not with the same level of trust and care that's developed in person. Nothing can replace getting to know someone face-to-face."

"I understand that, Oscar. But people have less and less time these days because there's so much competing for our attention."

"And you've just beautifully articulated why nothing will ever replace face-to-face conversation. When you and I have our conversations, we have each others' complete attention. We're unconsciously aware of each others' facial expressions, eye and body movements, and breathing. One's physiology has a way of informing a conversation far more accurately than words alone ever will."

Oscar gestures by waving his hands about as he passionately argues his point. "We're physical beings in a physical world. It's true that physical beings can accomplish many wonderful things that weren't possible prior to the digital age. But it's not possible to build an authentic relationship strictly through virtual interaction. And even if it were, you'd be very unhappy being cooped up in front of a computer, networking with virtual people, instead of being out in the world with real people."

"I suppose you're right about that."

"But again, such technology can most definitely be used as a vehicle for finding the right people to hang out with."

"So if you were me, how would you use it to find the right people?"

"First, I'd make sure that anything I did maintained the integrity of the hanging out philosophy."

"You mean it has to serve others and leave them better than they were before they connected with me?"

"Exactly! Next, I'd settle upon an online platform that specifically caters to the business community."

"You mean something like LinkedIn?"

"That's one example. However, the advancement of communication technology is so fluid in your age that whatever today's standard is may be obsolete in a couple of years. Think about it, most of what's considered the state-of-the-art in virtual networking technology today didn't even exist five or ten years ago. And what was considered the standard platform five or ten years ago is either obsolete or doesn't even exist anymore. Therefore, what system you use isn't anywhere near as important as how you use it. That means embracing the philosophy of service and exercising reasonable caution."

"What do you mean by exercise reasonable caution?"

"When sowing your garden online, it would be wise to assume everyone is a weed, or a hunter seeking prey, until they prove to you otherwise."

"I'm not sure I understand."

"Weeds and hunters are attracted to the online world because it's easy to mask one's true agenda by simply manufacturing a well-worded profile. Therefore, I'd like to share with you a simple online strategy for finding the right people to network with. You may want to write this down."

I flip to a new sheet of paper, then nod that I'm ready.

"First, create an online profile that filters those who attempt to connect with you. Your profile should clearly state that you don't use that particular social media platform for casual contact, and that you don't connect with anyone online that you haven't met."

"How do I say that without coming off as standoffish?"

"Try this. It's off the cuff, but you can tweak it.

> *I don't use (name of social media platform) for casual acquaintances. I only connect with those whom I have met in person, or who have been referred to me by a trusted member of my network. This keeps the integrity of my network high and maintains the trust others have in me as a valuable referral source. If you don't have my phone number, send me a message about why you want to connect and to schedule a time to meet. I'm always happy to get together with you in person to learn more about you, your business, and discover how we might network with each other.*

"You can either place this in the body of your profile or, if there's a section on the profile specifically designated for instructions on how to connect with you, place it there."

I raise an eyebrow as I finish writing the message.

"You've got a problem with that message?"

"That does sound standoffish. I might be resistant to connect with someone if I saw that message on their profile."

"Would you really? Even if they were a trusted member of your network or had been referred to you by a trusted member of your network?"

"Hmmm . . . In that context, I guess I might actually respect such a message. Okay, I get it. It's a message that creates respect from those who genuinely want to get to know me and filters out the casual connectors."

"Exactly. Remember, you're a networker. You're not a marketer trying to collect as many names as possible to add to your database or to impress people with how many connections they have. Nor are you a job hunter who's trying to impress potential employers with the number of connections you have.

"As a networker, you only connect with those that you know and trust, and who share the hanging out philosophy. Such discrimination will establish your online reputation as a serious networker, and will attract those who are in alignment with the philosophy of service."

"I get it! This makes it easy to find those whom I really want to meet and allows me to keep out the weeds."

Oscar replies with an affirmative wink and proceeds. "Now, once you've created your profile, invite only those with whom you already have a trusting relationship into your online network. Once you're connected, you can see who's in *their* network that you would like to be introduced to.

"Don't attempt to connect to those people yet," he says, pointing a cautionary finger at me. "Instead, ask the trusted members of your network for an introduction. If a physical meeting with those people you want to meet is possible, schedule it. Have a hang out and get to know them just as you would someone you met at a networking event."

"This is great, Oscar. But what if hanging out with them isn't possible?"

"Then you have to evaluate whether or not this is someone you really want to connect with, and why. Here's a useful rule to follow: if connecting to an individual virtually is your only option, but doing so allows you to serve them and others in your network, then you should by all means establish that relationship."

"So it's a matter of keeping a balance between connecting with those whom I really want to meet and keeping out the weeds?"

"Exactly. Just be diligent in keeping out the weeds. Weeds love to connect online with those they have no previous relationship with, and they tend to do so by posing as a connection with someone in your network. When those you don't know attempt to connect with you, it's important to quickly find out if they're a fellow gardener, or just a weed trying to invade your garden."

"How do I find that out?"

"When someone you don't know invites you to connect, look to see with whom in your network they're connected to. Then call that mutual connection directly and ask them how well they know this stranger who's trying to connect with you. You'll be amazed at how often they won't even recognize the name. If that's the case, it means you've probably been contacted by someone who uses online networking casually."

"So that means they're a weed?"

"No, it just means they use online networking casually. You, however, operate by a different standard. It's important that you maintain that standard. Therefore, I recommend that you reply to anyone who's attempting to establish an online connection to you with the following message. You might want to keep this handy so it's easy for you to cut and paste into an e-mail reply. Ready?"

"Hold on. I might as well just type into a text file in my laptop right now so I don't have to re-type it later." I open the text program on my laptop. "Okay, ready."

Oscar dictates the following message:

> *Dear So-and-So,*
>
> *Thanks for reaching out. As my online profile states, I only connect with those whom I personally know (have met face-to-face) or who have been referred to me by a trusted member of my network. This keeps the integrity of my network high and maintains the trust others have in me as a valuable referral source.*
>
> *How about getting together so we can learn more about each and discover how we might network together? Once we've determined we'd be suitable networking partners, I'll be happy to create a connection. Call me at 503-555-0912, and we'll set something up.*

"Oscar, that's a great message," I exclaim as I add my name to the end of the message. "It's not offensive, and it really lets people know I'm serious about my relationships. If I received a response like that, I'd be on the phone in a hot second to set up a meeting."

"Of course you would. But that's because you're a gardener. However, you may be surprised to learn that three out of four people won't respond. Those are the weeds who are just trying to rack up connections. But the one in four that does respond will, in almost every case, turn out to be a fellow gardener who'll become a good friend as well as a valuable networking partner."

"This is awesome! It's like using online networking as my own spiderweb that captures people to hang out with."

"I guess that's one way of looking at it."

~School's Out~

"Speaking of hanging out, I still have to make my follow-up calls from last night's mixer. Is there anything else we need to cover?"

"At this point, your assignment is to follow the instructions I've given you over the last few days. Do the job you're paid to do to the best of your ability, continue your studies in support of your financial service venture, and consistently practice the hanging out formula as time allows. And for goodness sake," he raises his voice and wags his finger at me, "stop trying the patience of your poor wife. I'll be back to check in on you. When I do, you should have some interesting results to report, and, I'm sure, many questions," he says with a pat on my back.

"So that's it. We're done?"

"School's out, kid. You have the formula. You know where and how to apply it, and you've had an opportunity to actually employ each of the lessons. Time to get your butt to work."

"But, Oscar, I don't have the money to join the chamber of commerce, or the bar association, or even buy coffee while I'm hanging out."

With an "Ah-ah-ah" he raises his palm to me like a cop stopping traffic. "Remember our first conversation? Embrace your situation for the gift it truly is."

"I know. I know. But the promise of the gift doesn't make skinny dipping through the sewer to get to it any easier."

"No, I suppose it doesn't. But wallowing in the sewer will only make the journey take longer and make you smell worse. So you'd better start swimming."

"This isn't fair, Oscar. I—"

"It isn't fair? Oh, poor baby," he interrupts by condescendingly patting my cheek.

Annoyed, I push his hand away. "Look, Karen's ready to have me thrown into a padded cell. You can't just leave me like this!"

He holds up his palms in a defensive gesture. "All right, all right. I suppose I'm at least partly responsible for that dilemma. I'll get you off the hook with your wife this time. But don't you be giving that poor girl any more reasons to be worried about you," he says pointing a stern finger at me.

"I want you to know this really is against policy," he says, grabbing my wrist before I can react. "And so it is," he bellows, making a sweeping gesture with his other hand.

I get a queasy sensation of falling, accompanied by a sound, like a fish bowl being placed over my head. Everything seems to be going out of phase.

-------- �֎ --------

The world gradually comes back into focus with a sound like I'm emerging from under water. I feel kind of woozy, as if I just had an attack of vertigo. I've somehow ended up across the table from Oscar.

"What, what the hell did you just do to me?"

"Like I said, gettin' you off the hook."

Everything is different. The people in the coffee shop have changed, but yet they all seem familiar. It's dark outside. On the table sits the brown sack of greeting cards I mailed last night. "What happened?"

"I think a more appropriate question would be what just un-happened." He looks around and whispers, "We took a short trip through curved space-time. Kinda cool, eh?" he says wagging his eyebrows.

"Huh?"

"I've returned you to exactly fourteen hours before our last moment in time. The incident with your wife being upset by your talking to the teapot hasn't happened. And it better not!" he scolds again, pointing his accusatory finger at me.

"It . . . it won't," I answer, completely freaked out by what has just transpired.

"With the exception of the lesson we just completed, the last fourteen hours of your life have yet to happen. Which means you still need to get those into the mail," he says pointing to the greeting cards neatly sealed, stamped, and stacked on the table, just as I remember them after we completed our lesson from last night. "Then get yourself home and get a good night's sleep tonight. And for goodness sake, don't upset the wife this time!"

"I . . . I will. I mean I . . . I won't," I stutter, still rattled.

Oscar scoots his chair back away from the table, stands to leave, takes one step, stops, and turns around, "Oh, and one more thing."

"What's that?"

"Hurry home and get your shirt in the wash before that mocha stain sets."

"What mocha? Oh no!" I suddenly remember the incident from before and am again jolted out of my chair by the familiar SPLORSH and the shock of the iced mocha running down my back.

"Oh my gosh! Oh my gosh! I'm so sorry."

"Oh, not again!"

Places to Find people to hang out with

Referral Groups

Look up local referral groups. When I hang out with people, mention that I'm looking for an introduction to one.

Some groups are better than others. Take my time to find the right one. Visit a group before joining to observe how they operate.

Notice who's in the group. Are they really in business or just dabbling? They should check me out before allowing me to join.
Hang out with a few members to get to know them.

Trust my feelings about the group. If it's a good group, I'll feel like the most important and welcome person in the room.

Service groups

Don't join for the networking. Participate because I believe in the causes that the group stands for and because I want to support that mission. Allow the networking to happen.

Think of it like fishing. Some networking might happen just like some fish might get caught.

Online Networking

1. Create a profile that states how I want to be contacted. i.e.

   I do not use (social media platform) for casual acquaintances. I only connect with those who I have met in person or who have been referred to me by a trusted member of my network. This keeps the integrity of my network high and maintains the trust others have in me as a valuable referral source.

   If you don't have my number, send me a message about why you want to connect and to schedule a time to meet. I'm always happy to get together with you in person to learn more about you, your business and discover how we might network or collaborate with each other.

2. Start by connecting with only the trusted members of my network.

3. See who they're connected to and ask for introductions. (Don't request a connection to them until after I've met them.)

4. Once we've been introduced, schedule a hang out and get to know them, just as I would someone I met at a networking event.

(IF hanging out with them isn't possible because of distance, have a phone conversation. IF it feels right, make an online connection)

5. It's OK to Connect with those I haven't met as long I'm sure they're not a weed, and doing so will serve them or others in my network.

6. IF someone I don't know invites me to link to them, First see who we know in common and ask that person if they can vouch For the one who's requesting the connection.

Weed out the hunters by sending the e-mail reply inviting them to hang out before we connect.

PART FOUR

SEVENTEEN

What Day is This?

I'm shivering under a bridge, my body wrapped in a muddy blanket, my last possession other than the same filthy clothes I've been wearing for I don't know how long. I've haven't worked in months. Karen left me after I was fired from my job and now I don't have a friend in the world.

Not long after he disappeared, I simply stopped believing Oscar ever existed. I convinced myself that the idea of hanging out for a living, and the formula he taught me, was all just a ridiculous theory cooked up by the same mental illness that had me believing I was being mentored by a fat, millennia-old chariot builder. Paralyzed by self-doubt, I gave up on everything and fell into depression.

An icy wind bites at my ears. I try to draw my body as close in on itself as I can to keep warm, trembling from the wet, frigid weather. Voices in my head argue about which is worse, the cold and hunger or the loneliness and shame.

Footsteps accompanied by an unsympathetic yet familiar voice break through the sound of windswept rain slapping the pavement. "Poor baby." The words echo off the soot-covered cement walls supporting the underpass. I look up and just catch the backside of a rotund figure passing by. "Poor, poor baby," the voice says again as the figure fades from view.

"Oscar, wait," I wheeze, reaching out with the grimy tips of my fingers that are poking through holes cut in the end of a sock covering my hand for warmth. "Please don't leave."

"Poor, poor baby," the voice reverberates as it seems to dissolve into the distance.

"Yes he is. He's just a poor baby, isn't he? You silly kitty."

I surface from the frightening dream, finding myself in bed next to Karen, who is playing with Baxter.

"It was a dream! Oh, thank God it was just a dream," I mumble struggling to reorient myself with my surroundings.

"Weird dream?" Karen asks as Baxter flies off the bed and out the bedroom door.

"Yeah. A horrible, weird dream."

"Want to tell me about it?"

"No, I just want to forget it. What day is this?"

"Wow, you really were out of it. Are you feeling okay?"

"Yeah, the headache's gone," I answer, recalling that I turned in early last night after being hit with the first migraine I've had in nearly two weeks. In fact, the last one I had was the one in the car right before Oscar appeared.

Karen lays beside me and strokes my head. "It's Sunday. Remember, you promised we'd spend the day together. We're having a picnic lunch in the park, and then we're going to the matinee downtown."

"What time is it?"

"It's almost eight. You've been asleep for nearly ten hours, honey, and you needed it. That's the most sleep I've seen you get in weeks," she says, now rubbing my chest. "You're sure you feel all right?"

"Yeah, I'm just hungry."

She gives me a peck on the cheek, rolls off the bed, steps into the living room, and calls back, "That's good, because coffee's on, and breakfast'll be ready as soon as you're out of the shower. I'm making pancakes and sausage."

"Oh boy!" I exclaim, throwing back the covers and feeling just as hungry as I did in the dream. Karen is an amazing cook, but with our crazy schedules, I'm on my own when it comes to breakfast during the week. So Sunday breakfast is a special treat.

I place my feet on the floor and sit on the edge of the bed, pausing to process the strange nightmare. Relief that I'm not actually homeless and freezing under a bridge in a not-so-distant dystopian future is tempered by the reality that, if things don't improve soon, the dream could turn out to be a precognitive vision. The fear of losing everything and ending up destitute has been haunting me since my encounter with the homeless guy in Chinatown a couple of weeks back.

Karen deserves so much better than the situation I've put her in. Our financial circumstances have already tested our relationship past what I thought would be the breaking point. Yet there she is, making breakfast and looking forward to spending the day with me.

In no hurry to leave the bed, I sit on the edge and let myself slip into a sort of daydream, a disjointed replay of the past weeks' events.

It's been nine days since I last saw Oscar. In an attempt to avoid dredging up the conversation about him with Karen, I hid the teapot behind some blankets in the back of the linen closet. She and I have been doing a great job of pretending we never had that middle-of-the-night conversation, and I don't want to rock the boat by having it come up again. In fact, with each passing day, the unbelievable encounter with Oscar becomes easier and easier to dismiss as some kind of temporary psychotic episode. What I can't dismiss is the fondness I developed for him, or the fact that, real or not, I miss him. I've pulled the teapot out a couple of times since bringing it home, just for reassurance, but I no longer feel the electrical charge.

Career-wise, this past week has easily been the most fulfilling of my life, and also one of the most hectic. Since our last lesson, and the inexplicable temporal shift at the coffee shop in Powell's, I've followed Oscar's instructions exactly. I've hung out with fifteen people and enjoyed every moment. Eleven of them I met on my sales route. Two of those turned into Yellow Page sales, one for a $345 per month triple-quarter-column ad, my biggest sale yet! That puts me just under ten percent of the way to my sales goal, which I have less than two weeks to hit if I'm going to keep my job.

One of the guys I met at the Portland Business Alliance mixer, Brent, the owner of Krowten Payroll, came with me to the Slarrefer business opportunity meeting yesterday and signed up as my first distributor.

I also went to the Alliance Shop Talk mixer early Tuesday morning and met one person to hang out with, a property and casualty insurance broker. That was the second, and therefore last, alliance event I'm allowed to attend as a guest. I really want to join, but just don't see how I can scrape the $400 membership fee together.

I had a delightful conversation with Moira at the bar association on Thursday, and she assured me I'd be welcome into the association. Membership is $150 that I can't afford to invest, but realize I can't afford not to invest. I stalled by telling her I wanted to get it cleared with Slarrefer before I made a commitment to join.

Most important, I've already been able to make some potentially valuable introductions. Even though he's not a potential client or referral source, I spent an hour with Marv, the executive director of Portland Home Care, learning about him and his company. He sent me an e-mail thanking me profusely for the introduction to Nadia and Anton. He said they were already discussing referring business to each other. Never once during our conversation did he ask anything about me or my business. But his thank-you note was all I needed to make me feel the meeting was well worth it. I'm really beginning to get what hanging out in service to others means.

Between all that hanging out, making the office meetings at work, attending the evening classes for Slarrefer, and squeezing in my studies, I'm exhausted. Karen insisted I take today off just to spend with her. I feel like I've earned a break. Besides, we don't have any problems I can do anything about until tomorrow anyway, so today belongs to us.

"Hey, what're you doing in there? Breakfast is almost ready," she yells from the kitchen.

With a yawn and a stretch, I rise to my feet and stumble into the bathroom. "Be there in a minute."

EIGHTEEN

The Referral

"Tyler, this Nadia."

"Hey, Nadia," I answer, holding the phone between my ear and shoulder while trying to tie my shoe. It's seven-thirty, a full hour before the Monday morning sales staff meeting. I'm scrambling to get to the office at least half an hour early. Of the five of us who were hired in June, I'm the only one who hasn't hit at least eighty percent of the probationary revenue goal. Though the chances of hitting my quota by Friday of next week, the day probation ends, is about the same as hitting the lottery, I still have two weeks salary coming to me (as long as I don't do anything to get terminated early). I'm on such thin ice that even something like showing up without a tie would be enough to get me fired, so I want to make extra sure I show up to every meeting on time.

"I'm sorry for calling so early. Hope I didn't catch you at a bad time."

"I'm just getting dressed to get to a meeting. What's up?"

"Well, first, Papa and I want to thank you so much for introducing us to Marv. He's decided to use us as the preferred medical supplier for Portland Home Care!"

"Nadia, that's wonderful!"

"Yes, we are very excited. Also, our friend Stan wants to talk to you about advertising in your Yellow Page directory."

"What's Stan's business, Nadia?" I ask, distracted by Baxter rubbing his head against my shoe and swatting at the laces.

"He's a personal injury attorney."

I have a hard time paying attention as I try to hold the phone, tie my shoe, and wrestle with Baxter. "Nadia, I'd love to talk with him. I'm in kind of an awkward spot right now. Would you mind e-mailing his information to me along with any details you think I should know."

"I'd be happy to. And thanks again so much."

"Thank you, Nadia. I'll give Stan a call soon as I can. You have a great day!"

"You too, Tyler. Bye."

I raise my head, let the phone drop onto the bed, shoo Baxter away, and finish tying my shoe. "Stupid cat," I mumble while trying to brush the white fur off my black shoes and trousers.

Fearing I might be late, I frantically run to the kitchen to get the pet hair roller. I roll the sticky spool over my trousers, then run back into the bedroom to pick up my phone and briefcase, then back to the kitchen to grab an apple from the fridge, and finally to the door where Baxter is waiting to be let out. "Meow" he demands, telling me to hurry up, he's tired of waiting. As soon as I turn the knob, he squirts out the door and disappears down the stairs. I quickly lock up, following close behind.

~Elasgib & Freeman~

It's nine thirty, and the office is filled with post-meeting commotion. I'm sitting at a desk reading Nadia's e-mail.

> *Tyler,*
>
> *Please give Stan Elasgib a call at 503-555-9361. We saw him over the weekend and told him about you. I showed him our ad proof. He wants to find out about running an ad for his firm and is expecting your call.*
>
> *Nadia*
>
> *P.S. Thanks again for introducing us to Marv!*

I immediately give Stan a call.

"Elasgib and Freeman. How may I direct your call?" says a woman's voice at the other end.

"This is Tyler Cirella with Yellow Page USA. I'm trying to reach Stan Elasgib. I understand he's expecting my call."

"One moment, please."

After listening to hold music for more than a minute, a voice comes through the line. "This is Stan."

"Hi, Stan. This is Tyler Cirella with Yellow Page USA. I was told by Nadia Gagosian to give you a call."

"Yes, Tyler, thanks for reaching out so promptly. I'm looking to expand my advertising footprint. Would it be possible to meet with you this week?"

"Other than late this afternoon, I'm completely booked out for the rest of the week, Stan. Can I swing by this afternoon around four?"

"Four o'clock today would be perfect. We're in Lincoln Center, tower one, top floor."

"Wonderful, Stan. I'll see you then."

I hang up and look at the time: 9:20. My first appointment is at eleven. I quickly make two calls confirming todays' appointments, and then begin my investigation of Elasgib and Freeman to see what kind of advertising they already have. I comb through the competing directories, stored in the office just for this purpose, and discover a half-page ad in one directory and a full page, full color ad on the back cover of the telephone company directory. That is the single costliest ad in the industry. I gulp at the possibility of landing a very big account.

I plug my laptop into the desk terminal, run to the office printer, scan the ads, send the files to my laptop, and run back to the desk. Over the course of the next thirty minutes, I create a sample ad formatted for the Yellow Page directory. Just as I'm putting on the finishing touches, I cringe at the sound of Glenn's voice behind me.

"What's this?" he asks, leaning over my shoulder.

"It's an ad mock-up, Glenn. Look, I'm really in a hurry. Do you mind?" I press *print* on my laptop and stand to run back to the printer, but Glenn is blocking my path.

"You gotta be kidding. You think you're gonna get Elasgib and Freeman?"

"Please leave me alone, Glenn." I push my way past him and dash to the printer.

"I'll give two reasons why you're wasting your time," he calls out. "One, that's my territory, and two, I tried selling them an ad. They're not interested."

I snatch the copies from the printer and quickly glance at them to make sure they look okay, and reply, "Thanks for the warning." I run back to the desk, pack my laptop and the ads into the briefcase, and rush out of the office to my eleven o'clock appointment.

"Tyler, pleasure to meet you," Stan Elasgib greets me as he emerges from a doorway leading into the back. It's four fifteen, and I've been nervously twiddling my thumbs for the last twenty minutes in the office waiting room.

"Sorry to keep you waiting. I was on a call with counsel for an insurance company we're opposing in a lawsuit. Can I get you anything? Coffee?"

"Herbal tea if you have it. Otherwise just water would be fine."

"Suzy, can you please bring Tyler here an herbal tea, and I'll have the usual."

The receptionist pokes her head through the reception window. "We have mint, orange pekoe, passion fruit, lemon ginger—"

"Lemon ginger sounds great," I interrupt.

"Please, come into my office," Stan says, motioning with his hand. I follow him through a pair of large wooden doors into an office with a breathtaking, one-hundred-eighty-degree view of the green rolling hills that serve as background to the communities of Lake Oswego, Tigard, and the southwest side of Portland. Floor-to-ceiling mahogany bookshelves filled with law books line the walls. A space about six feet wide behind a beautiful huge matching mahogany desk displays several awards and certificates surrounding a centerpiece diploma from Stanford Law School.

He motions for me to take one of the two seats in front of the desk and seats himself in a large, black leather executive office chair. "Thanks for coming out on such short notice. I'd been considering advertising with your directory for some time, but after a rather unpleasant encounter with another one of your other sales reps, I've been holding off."

Already feeling quite intimidated by the surroundings, Stan's comment makes me feel especially uncomfortable. I know he must be talking about Glenn, and I'm not surprised, given some of the other stories I've heard. *So why am I here?* I wonder.

"I'm terribly sorry you had an unpleasant experience, Stan. How can I help you?"

"You know, in my field, I often get labeled as an ambulance chaser because of a few bottom feeders in our industry. After talking with Nadia and Anton, it occurred to me that my opinion of your company may have been unfair, and that, perhaps, I just ran into a bad rep."

"Well, I certainly hope I can change your mind about us."

"I hope you can too. I'd rather not go into the detail, but your associate who dropped in here a month or so back made a very poor impression upon our receptionist, Suzy. He came back a second time when I was here and—" He hesitates as if to choose his words carefully. "Maybe it's just the business I'm in, but I can smell a snake."

"Stan, you and I both know that Yellow Page USA has been around for some time. We wouldn't be in business if whomever you met was an accurate reflection of how we conduct business."

"And that's why I wanted to meet you. I was at Nadia and her parents' home for dinner Saturday night, and they described your rather unique approach to business. She also showed me your directory. I really am interested in expanding our advertising, but I'd rather work with someone who cares and does the right thing."

"I'm honored to have the chance, Stan. So how do you know Nadia and Anton?"

"I've had some business dealings with Anton's cousin down in Southern California, and he asked me to help them relocate to Portland. They're very sweet people."

"They certainly are. So who do you want to attract with your ad, Stan?"

After he explains that he specializes in accident cases involving commercial vehicles, I give Stan my presentation and share the Portland area directory with him. He practically drools over the mock-ups I've created and agrees to purchase a full page, full color ad in the attorney classification.

"So what do I have to do to get this spot?" he asks while examining the back cover of the current book, which displays an ad for a competing law firm.

"I'm afraid existing advertisers have first right of refusal, Stan. That's prime real estate, and they're not about to give it up."

"All right, we'll just do this full page thing. What can you do for me?"

I examine the pricing chart and have to fight to keep my composure. A full page ad runs $3,500 per month. I also have the authority to offer him an additional half page at no additional cost, which I'll use as leverage to get the deal done.

I get out my calculator and compute the annual revenue, although to Stan it just looks like I'm running the numbers for the cost of the ad. The figure I arrive at is $42,000. With the sales I've already made, this will put me at just over $47,000 in annual revenue. Still short of my $55,000 revenue goal, but the eight percent commission on this sale alone would be over $3,000, the equivalent of an additional six weeks of straight salary.

"The price is $3,500 per month for a full page, full color ad. If we can get the contract done this week, I can throw another half page, or two quarter pages in another classification, into the package."

"Really? I'll take that deal. But, you know, I really hate having to deal with a monthly bill. Can I just pay for the whole year?"

I'm biting my tongue to keep from screaming. A contract turned in with full payment increases my commission by fifty percent. *Play it cool*, I think.

I take a swig of my now cold tea and clear my throat. "Sure. In fact, I can knock one month off the price if you do."

"Great. Let's set a time to have you come back with the necessary paperwork and, if everything checks out, I'll sign the contract and have Suzy draw up a check."

We decide I'll return with the revised mock-ups and the contract on Wednesday at noon, which means having to re-schedule a hang out I have on the calendar at that time. It's a small price to pay for a sale this size. As I step out the door to leave, I remember one critical detail, "Oh, Stan, one more thing."

"What's that?"

"You're not in my sales territory. For me to get credit for this, it's going to have to be approved by my manager. I'll explain to her that you were referred to me by Nadia and Anton, but I'm pretty sure my associate who you encountered earlier is going to object and try to claim this as his sale because it's in his territory. If it becomes an issue—"

"If it becomes an issue," he interrupts, "just have your manager give me a call. I'll not only explain that I'm working with you, but that if they try to reassign my account to that other jerk, I'll withdraw my ad."

"Thanks, Stan," I gulp. "See you Wednesday."

I climb into the Saturn and recalculate the sales figures. Because Stan is going to pay for the year up-front, that drops the revenue total down to $38,000. The good news, though, is that the commission on a paid-in-full sale is twelve percent. "Forty-six hundred and twenty dollars! Yahoo!" I scream. "That'll take some pressure off."

I check the time: 5:30. I decide the best thing to do is just call Jan and explain the situation. After leaving a message, I head home. Just as I pull into my parking spot, my phone buzzes. The caller ID tells me it's Jan returning my call.

"Hey, Jan."

"What do you need, Tyler?" She sounds annoyed.

I explain the situation with Elasgib and Freeman, and do everything I can to avoid implicating Glenn. Although I can't stand him, I don't want to be the cause behind anyone getting into trouble. Besides, there's something about him that makes me believe he might be capable of seeking revenge.

"Okay, Tyler. Just so you know, I'm going to have to run this by Glenn. This account is in his territory. I have to find out whether or not he visited this office, and if so, why he didn't make the sale."

"I understand. The client said if it's an issue that you should just call him. See you tomorrow for the phone-a thon."

"See you then. Bye."

My excitement gives way to a horrible feeling in the pit of my stomach. If Jan calls Stan, she's going to get an earful. One of two things will happen. Stan will cancel the sale and everyone loses, or I'll get the credit, and Glenn will be upset with me.

"Even if I get the credit for the sale, I'm still over ten grand $10,000 short of my revenue goal. So next Friday's going to be my last day in any case," I tell myself with a shrug. I lock the car and make my way up the stairs, pondering whether or not to say anything to Karen about the pending sale. Given my luck, and the volatility of the situation, I decide it would be best to wait until Wednesday when I have the check and contract in hand. No point in getting her hopes up just in case the sale ends up falling through.

~I'm Gonna Get You, Cirella!~

"It's three thirty on Tuesday afternoon, and I'm in the middle of setting an appointment. I hear arguing, then Jan's office door slamming loudly. I'm wearing a headset, so it's only slightly distracting. As the call ends, I remove the headset and am confronted by an enraged Glenn peering over the partition from the adjoining cubicle. "I don't know what you said to turn that attorney against me, Cirella, but you have no right to come into my territory and steal my clients."

"Outside, Glenn, or I'm calling security!" Jan yells from her office door. The entire office falls into a stunned silence.

"I'm gonna get you, Cirella," Glenn whispers, then grabs his briefcase and blazer and storms out of the office.

"Tyler, I'd like to see you in my office," Jan calls out. I'm dreading this moment. I have no idea how this conversation is going to go, but just the thought of having it reinforces my intense dislike for this job.

"Close the door and take a seat," she orders. I sit down in the same chair I was in when she suggested I quit a couple of weeks ago. I look out the window at the Portland skyline, wishing I was anywhere out there rather than in here. Jan's office reminds me of my grade school principal's office. Being in here can mean only one thing: trouble.

"Glenn claims you somehow sabotaged his relationship with that attorney you met with yesterday so that you could steal the sale."

I don't answer. The accusation doesn't deserve an answer. Even though it's so ridiculous it's almost funny, it really angers me.

"However," she continues, "I called this Stan fellow. According to him, Glenn made a very poor impression. He also explained how you and he happened to connect. Tyler, he's very impressed with you. And if your clients are raving about you like the ones who referred you to him are, perhaps it means I've misjudged you."

"I don't think you misjudged me, Jan. It was explained very clearly in training that your decision to keep or fire probationary employees is based on the numbers. I haven't been making mine."

She gives me a kind of empty stare, like she's not sure what to say next. "Well, this sale is yours to lose. You feel like you can handle it yourself?"

"Sure. He's already agreed to the ad copy, I just have to print out the mock-ups and bring them to him tomorrow with the contract."

"All right, then, good luck. If you need anything call me." She puts her glasses on and turns to her computer. "That'll be all," she says, abruptly ending the conversation.

I stand to leave, but have to stop and ask, "So, what about Glenn?"

She peers over her glasses at me. "He's my concern, Tyler," she says with no emotion whatsoever, returning her attention back to the monitor.

How much rope does this guy get? I ask myself as I leave Jan's office, wondering if I'll find my tires slashed when I get back to the car.

~*Show Me the Numbers*~

"Have you had lunch?" Stan asks as he takes the contract and ad copy sheets from my hand. It's shortly before noon on Wednesday. I'm so nervous that the thought of food is the furthest thing from my mind.

"Not yet."

"We're ordering in. Would you like to join us? I think you may be here a little while."

"Sure, Stan. Thanks."

"Suzy, can you order a sandwich platter from the deli? And let Rick know Tyler with Yellow Page USA is here," he says into a telephone intercom.

"I'm on it," Suzy answers back.

"Glad to see you back, Tyler," he remarks while his eyes dart back and forth over the ad mock-ups. "Guess that nice chat I had with your manager yesterday straightened things out."

"Yeah, looks like I'm your sales rep."

"About that," he says as he drops the paperwork onto the desk. "I think we need to revise what we discussed."

"Here we go," I think to myself, not at all surprised. I knew landing a full page, full color ad was too good to be true. Thank goodness I didn't say anything to Karen.

"I was browsing this sample book you left and noticed this sentence here." He pushes the directory across the desk to me, keeping his finger where he wants me to read.

To order directories from another region please call
800-555-3589

"What other regions does your company publish directories in?"

"We pretty much cover the whole US," I answer.

"Am I not allowed to advertise in regions outside of our home office?" ·

"Of course. You can advertise anywhere you're licensed to practice law."

"Were you trying to hide that fact from me?" he asks with a sarcastic chuckle. "Seems to me it would be part of your job to inquire about any additional advertising our firm might need beyond the local book."

I gulp. He's right. I never did ask. I was so flustered about the idea of actually selling a full page ad that it never even occurred to me to show him any of the surrounding directories. "I'm . . . I'm sorry Stan. You're absolutely right. I should have shown you what other options you have. What other areas are you interested in?"

"We have an office in Eugene. We'd like to expand our advertising footprint from there up to Southwest Washington. Over the next three years, we're planning to open new offices in Medford, Olympia, and Seattle. Eventually I'd like to serve the entire I-5 corridor from Ashland to the Canadian border."

I feel faint at what Stan is proposing. Trying to keep my composure, I do my best to respond matter-of-factly. "We can do that."

"Show me the numbers. And if any of those directories have a back cover available, I want it."

"It's going to take some time for me to check those directory rates."

"You can use the conference room. Hopefully you'll have something for me by the time lunch arrives."

He directs me to the adjacent conference room where I take a seat, open my brief-case, and retrieve my calculator and rate card. Five of the directories Stan wants to advertise in currently have open sales campaigns. One of them has a back cover available. The rate for that ad alone is $5,000 per month, or $55,000 in annual revenue if he pays in full. That's the exact figure needed to make my quota. My mouth goes dry as I arrive at the total figure. Up until now, my biggest sale was $345 per month, and that client made a point of complaining about what a sizable investment that was.

After about twenty minutes, Stan pokes his head into the conference room. "Lunch is here. How're you doing?" he says, startling me.

I can't keep from stuttering. "There . . . there are f-f-five open books in the region that I can get you into right now, Stan."

"Let's discuss the numbers over lunch with my partner, Rick."

"Tyler, this is my partner Rick," Stan says as we step back into his office and take a seat at a round table in the corner.

"Pleasure to meet you, Rick," I say as I extend my hand. He shakes it and replies with a nod.

"Stan shoves a paper plate and plastic ware wrapped in a napkin in front of me. "Dig in," he says, motioning toward the platter of cold cuts and sandwich fixings. "So what're we looking at?" he asks as I load my plate. Rick, a deceptively quiet man, sits with an expectant expression as he bites into his sandwich.

I try to appear calm, but I'm so nervous at the size of this sale I'm not sure I can speak. "The whole program," my voice squeaks, "for one year, including the back page for the Salem book, the bonus ads, the online program, and figuring in the discount for paying in full," I say, feeling my eyelid begin to twitch uncontrollably, "is $93,500."

They look at each other. "One Williams case would take care of that," Stan says to Rick.

"In spades," he responds with a seemingly disinterested shrug and nods back at Stan.

"One Williams case?" I nervously inquire a couple of octaves above my normal vocal range.

"That's a case we settled a couple of months ago, a traffic accident involving a semi and a gal in a Honda. She'll never be able to walk again. She was awarded $2,900,000. Our fee is thirty percent, so it doesn't take many cases to give us decent return on an ad campaign like this."

Stan glances at his watch. "How much time do you need to write this up? I have an appointment at three."

"Another forty-five minutes at most to complete the contract and copy sheets. Then I should be ready for your signature."

Stan leans back, puts his feet up on the desk, and takes a bite of his pickle. "Let's do it."

~Look at Cirella's Numbers!~

It's shortly after three o'clock. I'm standing at the sales board in the office. We're required to post our sales each day. Anytime I post numbers it's an event, since I so rarely do so. Ads in five books, including one back cover and the online program, all count as separate sales that have to be posted individually. That means I have a lot of writing to do on the board. The marker squeaks as I scribble. Behind my back I hear a minor commotion begin to build.

"No way," a voice whispers. "Look at the numbers Cirella's posting!" says another. "Holy cow!" says yet another. Linda, the one person in the office who's not only been pretty nice to me throughout my short time at Yellow Page USA, but who has been both sympathetic and encouraging, runs up to the board. She's also not very happy working here, and has decided I'm the only person in the office she can relate to. "Oh my gosh, Tyler. This is wonderful!"

"Thanks, Linda," I reply, becoming a bit distracted by the reaction of my peers.

Jan emerges from her office, approaches the sales board, and gapes at the numbers. "I want to review that contract before it goes in the night pouch."

"I'll bring it in as soon as I'm done, Jan."

She starts to her office, stops at the door, and calls back out, "And Tyler?"

"Yes?"

"Congratulations."

~This Is a Celebration~

It's just after nine in the evening, and I'm trying to unlock the apartment door while Baxter, who's been waiting impatiently to be let inside, slithers between my legs like a furry snake. "Scoot puss!" I snap while trying to juggle my keys, briefcase, and the bag containing a bottle of champagne I picked up on the way home.

I've just returned from my Wednesday evening class at Slarrefer, and can't wait to share the news about today's sale with Karen. I've calculated that my commission will be $11,220. After taxes, I figure I'll see about eight grand of that. It doesn't get us out of all our financial problems, but it'll keep me from having to file bankruptcy, and it'll give us some breathing room. And, provided Stan sees a return on his advertising dollars, I can be reasonably sure he'll buy ads in more books in the coming months.

"I'm home," I call out.

Karen emerges from the bedroom in a robe with her head in a towel. "How was your day, honey?" she asks apprehensively. She knows I'm just days away from the end of my probation. And as far as she knows, I'm nowhere close to reaching my quota, so her concern is understandable.

I decide I'm going to milk this for all it's worth. I give her the most defeated expression I can muster up and let out a sigh. "Honey, I'm afraid I have some news."

She walks to the couch, crams herself into a corner, curls her legs underneath, and hugs a throw pillow. I just wanted to tease her a little, but she looks like she's going to burst into tears. Cruelly, I continue the charade. "I got some news about work today," I tell her while pulling a couple of wine glasses and a corkscrew from the cupboard. Holding them behind my back, I pick up the sack with the champagne, turn out the kitchen light, and walk over to the couch. The anguish on her face tells me to cut the act and give her the good news. If she holds that pillow any tighter, it's going to burst.

I place the glasses on the coffee table and remove the bottle from the sack. "What's this?"

"This is a celebration, my dear," I reply as I unwrap the foil and begin to twist the cork. "I made a little sale today."

She loosens her grip on the pillow. "And what exactly is a little sale?" she asks.

I pop the cork, trying not to let the foam get all over everything, and begin to pour.

"Tyler, what happened? What sale?" she starts to whine, shaking the pillow. I hand her a glass, forcing her to let go, and with a loud *tink* tap it with mine.

"A $93,500 sale!" I yell.

She gasps and sets her glass on the table. "Get out!"

"Paid in full," I add as I bring the glass to my lips. "After taxes, my commission should be just around eight grand."

She grabs my hand. "Okay, Tyler, is this for real? You haven't been seeing the fat genie guy again have you?"

"Oh, it's for real," I reply confidently. "This sale not only means I'll get to keep my job, but that I'll be able to us get on the Yellow Page group insurance plan!"

"Tyler!" she screams, lunging forward with a huge hug, practically knocking the glass out of my hand. "How did you land a $93,000 sale?"

I recount the story, beginning with Nadia's phone call Monday morning. I can't help but give credit to the formula Oscar taught me. However, I'm careful not to mention any of the supernatural details again.

"Not the guy in the teapot again. Tyler, you don't really expect me to believe any of that do you?"

"I don't care if you do or not. Sweetie, none of this would have happened if it weren't for his coaching, and I feel like I've barely scratched the surface of what's possible. It's weird. All I've been doing is meeting people, hanging out with them, learning about them, and then doing what I can to help them. Now I have my first Slarrefer distributor, I'm actually making Yellow Page sales, and I'm making friends along the way. It's like I'm . . . "

"It's like you're what?"

"It's like I'm hanging out for a living."

PART FIVE

Nineteen

Tests

It's a late October Wednesday afternoon. Karen took the day off to accompany me to the Brain Institute at the Oregon Health and Science University for a series of diagnostic procedures to find out the cause of my migraines. I'm lying inside an MRI scanner, staring at a picture of a tropical beach, affixed just inches above my nose to the wall of the machine. I told the specialists everything about my encounter with Oscar. As a result, I've spent the last week being grilled by psychiatrists, behavioral neuroscientists, and today, a neurologist. I have a follow-up appointment with him as soon as I get out of this contraption. They still haven't found anything, and at this point, I've had just about enough of being poked, probed, scanned and running around in paper-thin backless hospital gowns.

The machine makes a racket as I try to relax and keep still. *Whrrr . . . bang. Whrrr . . . bang. Whrrr . . . bang.*

"How you doing in there, Mr. Cirella?" the technician asks through an intercom between the loud bangs of the machine.

I press the call button once to signal I'm okay.

"We still have about twenty-five more minutes to go. Just stay still and remember, if you need anything, press the button twice."

I press the button again to let him know I understand and return my attention to the picture, which appears to have been cut out of an old magazine.

The idea must be that if you're staring at a picture of a South Pacific paradise, it'll help you relax. That's not easy to do with your head strapped into something called a head coil, while lying inside a giant metal doughnut that sounds like it's being hit with a sledgehammer. As I stare into the picture, my mind wanders back to that hot, horrible day at the end of July when I accidentally knocked the teapot off the shelf in the Tea Zone. I get a chill thinking about the bizarre turn my circumstances took as a result.

Now that a couple of months have passed, I realize that it must have been some sort of stress-induced psychotic break that conjured up Oscar and the series of impossible events that I'd imagined. One of the specialists here suggested that I may have experienced some kind of emotional breakdown that rewired my brain, tapping into an unconscious brilliance that revealed the formula of hanging out for a living, just as brain injuries and traumatic events have been documented to unlock previously hidden talents, memories, or creativity in some people. I can live with that explanation a lot more easily than the other possibility, that there's a tumor or something rewiring my brain and causing the headaches.

Whrrr . . . bang. Whrrr . . . bang. Whrrr . . . bang.

I think about what would have happened if I hadn't broken down and dreamed up Oscar. I would have wasted the last days of my probation being thrown out of every business I walked into until I'd been fired from my job.

I never would have met Nadia and Anton, or Stan Elasgib, or Brent Walker, or Marv Fenster, or any of the dozens of other people I've hung out with over the last ten weeks. I would have given up my Slarrefer business, convincing myself I didn't have enough time, enough money, or enough resources, just like every other business venture I invested in but never did anything with.

I'm sure Karen would have left me by now, and wisely so. There's no reason for her life to be ruined by the financial and legal problems I created, which very nearly did drive me into hopeless depression and probably homelessness. It's scary to think how close I came to being that pathetic other me I saw cowering under a bridge in the frightening dream I had on that Sunday morning back in August.

Instead I'm here, and I'm excited about the future. Of course, I'm concerned about what all these tests might reveal. But I also know how fortunate I am to now have the insurance to pay for them.

Whrrr . . . bang. Whrrr . . . bang. Whrrr . . . bang.

I begin to think about all the people I've hung out and shared the formula with over the last several weeks. So many people, in fact, that I've gained a minor reputation as the guy who hangs out for a living. The practice has resulted in a fairly steady stream of clients for my day job at Yellow Page USA. I'm far from being the highest producer in the office, but I am in the top forty percent.

I finally completed my Slarrefer Mutual training, earned my certification, and can offer long-term care insurance. I've been receiving commissions, and I just earned my second promotion to Regional Coordinator. It's a title meaningless in terms of my function, but significant in terms of how much I'm paid: more than double in residuals and customer acquisition bonuses than when I started.

I love my Slarrefer business. All I do is hang out with people, allow them to ask me about what I do, ask them if they want to see something cool, and then show them a video. I sign up those who want to use the service, sponsor those who see the business opportunity, and then help them do exactly the same. I've sponsored nine people so far, and my downline has grown to thirty-two. At this rate, I should be able to quit my daytime job and go full-time with Slarrefer in about eighteen months, if not sooner. In the meantime, my day job is paying the bills and allowing me to get the medical attention I need. I've been living by the words, "Do the very best you can at whatever you do, even if it's not what you want to do."

Whrrr . . . bang. Whrrr . . . bang. Whrrr . . . bang.

My mind drifts into the scene in the picture. Tahiti, that's where I want to take Karen! Financially, things are definitely getting better. She and I are still living pretty lean while we pay down the credit cards, but I was able to renegotiate with the bank, and they dropped the lawsuit. After everything I've put her through, Karen deserves a vacation. I wonder what that would cost? Who cares? I'll just research it, and then work my butt off 'til I've saved up the money. It'll take some time, though. I just started making payments on a new car.

Whrrr . . . bang. Whrrr . . . bang. Whrrr . . . bang.

The Saturn finally died, dramatically giving up its life in a smoke-filled finale by throwing a rod during rush hour traffic while attempting to get me home from work one last time. Stranded without a car, I rang up Sherry, a car broker I'd met on my sales route, to find out what she could do for me. She was ecstatic to hear from me.

A couple of weeks earlier, she and I met for coffee, and she identified her golden egg as busy executives who don't have the time to shop for a car. I then introduced her to Luigi, an elderly but spry Italian immigrant who relocated to Portland from Staten Island. He advertises himself as a mobile tailor. His golden egg is busy executives who don't have time to shop for clothes. As it turns out, it was a match made in heaven, and they're in the process of forming a referral group of mobile professionals who specifically serve busy executives. In fact, they're looking for a doctor who'll make house calls to join them.

I explained to Sherry that I had to get a reliable car right away, but that I was on a tight budget. She called me the next day to let me know she'd found a six-year-old, but very clean, Honda with eighty thousand miles on it. On top of getting me a great deal, she also bought a quarter page ad. My commission was just enough for the down payment.

Whrrr . . . bang. Whrrr . . . bang. Whrrr . . . bang.

Great, now my nose itches. Think of something else. Look at the picture. Oh yeah, Tahiti. It's a long flight, so we have to fly first class! A first class flight and a week, no make it two weeks, in Tahiti with Karen. Now that's something to work toward!

The voice over the speaker interrupts my thoughts. "Okay, Mr. Cirella, you're all done. Just hold tight, and I'll have you out of there in a minute."

~What's the Word, Doc?~

After parading around all afternoon in a backless hospital gown, I'm finally allowed to get dressed. I tuck my shirt in over the sound of three quick taps on the door, followed by the neurologist entering the examination room.

"What's the word, doc?" I ask.

"Until the MRI results come back from radiology, Mr. Cirella, I can't say for certain. The good news is that there's nothing remarkable about your CT scans, and all your other tests came back negative. However, I'm still quite concerned about the extended hallucinatory episode you described. You're sure you had no migraines during the time you experienced the hallucinations?"

"None, in fact, other than being worried that I was losing my mind, it was two of the most rewarding weeks I've ever had in my life. But a couple of days after Oscar disappeared, I started getting the headaches again. I've had two just this week."

He removes his glasses and gives me a concerned stare. "Well, there's nothing to suggest that the migraines and the apparition you experienced are related, but I'm not ruling anything out. May I walk you out to the waiting room?"

"Sure," I reply.

"As long as the sumatriptan is working for the headaches, I'm going to recommend that we do nothing else for the moment. I'd like for you to start keeping a diary of your headaches. Take notice of everything going on around you, what you ate, smells, even the weather," he says as we make our way through a maze of sterile white halls. "That's our best tool for discovering what may be triggering the headaches."

We reach the door into the reception area where Karen has been waiting. He allows me to pass while he remains in the doorway.

With a facial expression that reveals anguish and relief at once, Karen jumps up, grabs my hand, and pulls me close. "How are you, sweetheart?"

"I'm fine. They couldn't find anything wrong," I answer with a reassuring hug.

"Excuse me," the doctor interrupts. "Mrs. Cirella, may I speak to you alone for just a moment?"

"Of course, doctor," she answers, her expression now turning to all anguish.

"Umm, excuse me," I bark. "I have to get home to change. I'm serving as an ambassador at the Portland Business Alliance Green Hour mixer tonight, and I'm supposed to be there before five. What do you two need to talk about? I'm the patient."

"You just stay here and behave yourself. I'll be right back," Karen scolds.

I watch the door close behind them. The door has a viewing window allowing me to see the back of their heads as they talk in the hall. I pick up a magazine, let out a sigh, and grumble to myself, "I just wanna get outta here already."

After a few minutes they return. "Thank you, doctor," Karen says as they step back through the door into the reception room.

I toss aside the tattered *Time* magazine I've been skimming and lift myself from the chair. "You two done with your powwow?"

"Yes, we're done. He just wants me to make sure you keep up with your migraine diary."

She turns to the doctor. "Thank you again, doctor."

"Yeah, thanks again, doc," I say as I reach out to shake his hand.

"Best of luck to you both. We'll let you know soon as we have the results from the MRI."

We leave the office hand-in-hand, and by the time we make it outside we're arm-in-arm. It's unseasonably sunny and mild for mid-autumn. "Sure is warm for this time of year," I remark. Karen says nothing. It's obvious something's on her mind. Her left arm is wrapped around my right so tight I think I'm losing circulation. She obsessively pats my forearm as we walk to the parking structure.

"Sweetie, did that neurologist tell you something that he didn't tell me?" I ask.

"I don't think so, why?"

"Because you're holding onto me like you're afraid I'm going to float away." I look down at her hand stroking my arm. "And you keep petting my arm like you would a sick dog that you're taking to the vet to be put down."

"Oh, I'm sorry, baby," she says without loosening her grip. "The doctor told me all your tests came back normal. But he's still not ruling out the possibility that you may have something called a schizoaffective disorder that caused you to imagine the fat man."

"So he thinks I might be crazy?"

"He didn't say that. But he is concerned about those hallucinations, just like I am. He told me that if they return, it's extremely important that we get you back here immediately. He also told me to make sure you keep your migraine diary up to date."

She stops as we arrive at the car and looks me in the eye. "I'm just glad you're all right, sweetie. I've been so worried."

"Are you still worried?"

"No, not like I was before."

"Then may I have my arm back so I can unlock the car?"

She lets go, allowing me to retrieve my keys from my pants pocket. Before she can step around to the passenger side, I grab her arm, pull her close, and kiss her deeply on the lips. "Tell you what, how about we head back to the apartment and you can pet me all you want?" I say with a growl while waving my eyebrows at her.

"Stop that! We're in public!" she says, slapping me on the chest. "I guess you are all right. You silly thing, unlock this car!"

TWENTY

You Forgot Something

"Hey, Tyler, you mind if we head inside? I'm freezing."

It's just after three on Thursday afternoon. My tea companion, Alex, and I have been enjoying a chat outside the Tea Zone. When we sat down an hour ago, it was a balmy mid-seventies afternoon. But the late Indian summer has since given way to a blanket of clouds and a brisk wind, accompanied by a nearly twenty degree drop in temperature. Now the increasingly ominous sky threatens to bring more than just a nip in the air.

Alex, an arborist from Los Angeles, is in town for an arboriculture convention. I met him last night while serving as an ambassador at the Portland Business Alliance's Green Hour event. He was standing by himself, looking rather bewildered, so I offered to introduce him around. He's interested in expanding his business up here in Portland, and I'd like to grow my Slarrefer business down there, so we agreed that a meeting was in order.

We watch helplessly as the napkins on our table are snatched by a strong gust of wind and carried across the street. I slam my hand down on the networking profile I've been filling out just in time to keep it from being swept away too.

"I'm with you," I reply, gathering up my laptop and notepad.

We dash inside, settle into a corner table, and I return my attention to the referral profile. "So where were we?"

"I was telling you that my ideal client would be a hotel, golf course, resort, or a private estate in Southern California with palm trees on their grounds, takes pride in the appearance of their property, and are seeking an arborist they can contract with," he reminds me.

"That's your golden egg. Would you rather have the golden egg or the goose that lays the golden egg?"

"The goose, of course."

"Then we need to identify your goose. Who, by nature of their business, would have a network of hotels, golf courses, resorts, or private estates in Southern California?"

"That's easy, landscape architects for one. Oh my gosh, Tyler," he blurts out. "I get it! I've been banging my head against the wall trying to find anyone with trees when I should have been building relationships with landscape architects!"

"You're catching on. So do you know any landscape architects?"

"I know of a few, but they're minor acquaintances at best."

"If I were you, I'd start hanging out with them. You also need to identify your granny goose."

"My granny goose?"

"Yeah, your granny goose is that person or entity who would have a network of landscape architects or remodeling contractors."

"I know there's some kind of national landscape architects organization," he says while glancing at his watch. "Hey, Tyler, I really want to continue this conversation, but I've got about twenty minutes before I have to be on a conference call with my crew chief and office assistant. Do you think we could get together again? Your Slarrfer thing sounds like something I can use, and I'd like to know if there's anything I can do to help you make connections down in L.A."

"How long are you in town?

"I fly back Sunday afternoon."

Just as I'm about to suggest we meet back here over the weekend, the area behind my left eye begins to throb. Flashes of light start to erupt in the periphery of my vision.

"You all right, Tyler? All of a sudden, you don't look so good."

"It's a headache. They come on quick. I'll be fine." I retrieve a migraine pill from my briefcase, chew on it, and swallow it as fast as I can. It's a horrible tasting thing, but chewing the pills seems to get the medicine into my system faster.

"Can I call you tomorrow to set something up, Alex?" I ask. "I think I need to get going too."

"Sure."

"Thanks for coming in, guys," Janie says after we pay the tab and step out the door into a howling wind whipping through the street. The air smells burnt, and the sidewalk is polka-dotted from a momentary spritz of giant raindrops, a forewarning of wetter weather to come.

"Wow, the weather sure does change quick around here!" Alex shouts over the scraping sound of dry leaves being blown along the pavement by the roaring wind. "Which way do I go to get to the Mark Spencer hotel?"

"You want a ride, Alex? Looks like we're in for a soaker!" I shout back.

"Naw, I don't mind a little rain. We never get any weather in L.A., you know, so this is kind of interesting."

I don't know why I offered. The throbbing behind my left eye is beginning to spread. It's only a matter of minutes before I won't be fit to drive at all.

"The Spence is six blocks down," I answer, pointing south down Eleventh Avenue.

"Thanks, Tyler. You know, I really appreciate you having this conversation with me. It was worth the trip to Portland in itself," he says, shaking my hand.

"My pleasure, Alex. I enjoyed hanging out with you too."

"Are you sure you're okay?" he asks. "You're turning kind of green."

"Yeah, I'll be fine."

Actually, I'm growing nauseous, and the light out here hurts my eyes. Even in the gloom of the gathering storm clouds, I'm forced to squint.

"Well, feel better. I'll be waiting for your call tomorrow, and thanks again." He tucks his hands into his pants pockets and forges off into a vortex of swirling autumn leaves.

I know my parking stub is going to expire in just a few minutes, but I feel too lousy to deal with it. It's all I can do to step back into the Tea Zone for some dark shelter.

"Back so soon, Tyler?" Janie asks.

"Yeah, Janie. I've got a really nasty headache. You mind if I sit in the lounge?"

"Go ahead. I don't think anyone's back there now. But the happy hour crowd'll be coming in soon. Can I get you anything?"

"No, I get these once in a while. I just took a pill, but it takes a little while for it to work. Thanks."

I stagger into the mercifully dark lounge and seat myself in the corner. The familiar opening notes of Ravel's Bolero play softly over the sound system. My head pounds, and the aura around my field of vision pulsates in unison with the throbbing behind my eyes. I should call Karen to come get me and take me back to OHSU, but I just need to sit still. I lay my head down on my arms. Multicolored geometric shapes dance in the darkness of my closed eyes. "God, please make it stop."

The repetitive melody soothes me. I surrender to the music and drift off.

~The Operator's Manual~

The chaotic crescendo that finishes the Bolero jars me awake. I lift my head, rub my eyes, and blink. The headache is gone! It feels like I've been out for hours. I check the time: 3:37. I look around the room. The lounge is still empty. The strumming of a soft-jazz guitar now fills the room.

I make a mental note of everything that happened leading up to the headache so I can record it in my migraine journal. What I ate and drank, the abrupt change in the weather, and my location. I can write it down later. Right now I have to hurry to get to my car before parking enforcement does. I pick up my briefcase, scoot out from behind the table, and start for the door.

"You forgot something," an unmistakable voice calls out. I spin around and there, at the table where I was just seated, sits Oscar, waving my phone at me. I close my eyes for just a moment, and then open them. He's still there, wearing khaki olive pants, brown work shoes, and a light blue, short-sleeved work shirt. As usual, it's unbuttoned almost to the navel, revealing his hairy chest and belly. Also as usual, he's eating some kind of pastry with a cup of tea.

"Tylowitz! How ya doin', my boy?" he asks.

In spite of what Karen or the doctors would say about what I'm seeing, I'm overjoyed at the site of my dear friend and mentor.

"Oscar? Oscar, is it really you?"

He pats his face and pinches his arm. "Yeah, I'm pretty sure it's me."

I rush back, take the seat next to him, and can't help but stare with some disbelief. He breaks the pastry in two and offers me half. "Empanada?"

Overcome with emotion, I lean over and give him a hug without responding.

"Hey, hey, youse better take it easy," he protests in his gruff New York accent while reaching around and patting my back. "People might get the wrong idea."

I can't stop the tears from welling up in my eyes. "Where have you been? I nearly stopped believing I'd even actually met you."

"That's a helluva thing to say to your old friend!"

"I mean, well, you just disappeared, and I haven't seen a trace of you in nearly three months."

"I told you I'd be back to check up on you." He takes a bite and chews happily, like it's only been five minutes since we last spoke. "So how's life been treating you?"

Over the next several minutes I update Oscar on all that's transpired since our last meeting.

"So things are good with the wife?" he asks.

"They couldn't be better, Oscar. In fact, we've been talking about starting a family."

"Hey, that's wonderful, kid! Sounds like it'll be your turn to buy me a cigar before long."

"You know, Oscar, before you showed up, I couldn't imagine trying to support a family. Now everything's changed. None of this would have happened without your help."

"You're the one who's been climbing the mountain, kid. All I did was show you the way up."

"It goes deeper than that, Oscar. As important as getting back on track financially is, the best part has been the people I've met and the relationships I've formed. Hanging out for a living really is making friends for living."

"That was your original wish, wasn't it? To hang out with friends and make a living doing it."

"Yeah, but it's been even better than I could have expected."

"How so?"

"It's the philosophy. If I didn't understand the piece about hanging out in service to others, and thinking of networking in the same way I do gardening, the formula wouldn't work at all."

"And why do you suppose that is?"

"I guess because my expectations would have been different. Most of the people I've hung out with haven't actually referred anyone to me. And very few have actually become clients themselves. But since I never had that expectation, my business has grown in ways I didn't really expect."

"Oh, like how?"

"For example, there was Susan, this gal I met with who teaches Spanish. She works out of her house and gives private lessons. Her ideal clients are busy executives in the Portland area who want to learn Spanish so they can better communicate with associates and clients in Central and South America. I introduced her to my friend Patrick, who's expanding his consulting practice down there, and he signed up as her client. I also introduced her to the business editor of *El Hispanic News*, who I only know casually through the Portland Business Alliance.

She did send me an e-mail thanking me for the introductions, and told me that learning the formula was really helping her business. But she never bothered to ask anything about me or my business."

"So she didn't reciprocate?"

"That's the thing, Oscar. Thanks to you I didn't expect her to. But the garden did. Before I understood the philosophy of serving the garden, I would've been upset that she never even asked about me or my business. I would've told myself the formula doesn't work and that I'd wasted my time with her. But instead, I knew that helping her was simply serving the garden."

"So what happened?"

"I ran into the *El Hispanic News* business editor at an event, and he thanked me for making the introduction. Turns out she's sort of a goose for the paper. She bought a subscription and now assigns her clients to subscribe and read it as a homework assignment. Anyway, he asked me to meet him for coffee. When we met, he asked me a bunch of questions about my Slarrefer business, and I shared the granny goose formula with him. Long story short, it turns out he has a huge network of financial planners and accountants in the Latino community."

"So he turned out to be a goose?"

"Yeah. Anyway, he asked if one of his reporters could interview me for a story on effective networking. He offered to introduce me to some movers and shakers at the National Association of Hispanic Publications and the US Hispanic Chamber of Commerce. Oscar, that wouldn't have happened if I hadn't met with the Spanish teacher and done what I could to help her."

"Thanks for sharing that, kid," he says while leaning forward to give me a pat on the arm. "Your story demonstrates your mastery of the hanging out formula. When we first met, I was summoned forth on a wish that you could hang out for a living. That wish has been fulfilled. I've given you the formula, and it appears that you have been successfully employing it."

He pauses, lets out a sigh, and closes his eyes. This time it's not like he's gone into thought, but that he's resting. Slowly opening his eyes, he again breathes a deep sigh. He looks tired. Not an end-of-the-day tired, but a completely worn out kind of tired.

"Oscar, are you okay?"

"Yeah, I'm fine." He scratches his jaw while giving me a long, thoughtful look, as if he has something he wants to say but just can't find the right words. "It's just that the time has come for me to retire."

"I didn't know you could retire."

"Oh, yeah. The length of time one spends in extra-mortal servitude is the choice of the servant. Twenty-five hundred years is a long time to stay behind in the physical world. It's been a wonderful and rewarding journey, but I'm ready for the next chapter."

"What are you trying to tell me?"

"You're my last project, kid. I'll be living the rest of my days in this space-time."

"So that's it? You can give notice, and then just grow old and die like the rest of us?"

"You make it sound so macabre. I'm just going to finish out my physical life from the point when I first took possession of the teapot. Physically, I'm still only sixty-four years old. I'll probably have to cut down on the carbs, but I think I can squeeze another twenty years or so outta this carcass."

With another long sigh, he stretches out in the chair, crosses his feet, and folds his hands on his belly. "I'm looking forward to spending the rest of my days out here, rather than in that teapot until some schlub needs my help. Time to let my ticker wind down like everyone else."

"Oscar, have I done something wrong?"

"What do you mean?"

"Well, it seems pretty coincidental that you're retiring after working with me, and I don't see any other schlubs except me taking up your time. Did I . . . did I do something to make you want to quit?"

"Ha! Quite the opposite, kid. I guess my words came out wrong." He straightens up and leans toward me. "Remember, back at the cigar lounge, you asked me if there was anything you could do for me?"

"Yeah."

"Well, when one is empowered with extra-mortal servitude, they enter into a covenant which states, in part, that a suitable successor must be appointed before the position can be relinquished. It would make me very proud to have you as my successor."

"You, you want me to take over your job? Oscar, I'm still just a Yellow Page ad salesman. I live in a one-bedroom apartment, and I'm trying to work my way out of a mountain of debt. What do I know about helping people become successful?"

"Pretty much everything you need to know. You've demonstrated to my satisfaction that you have the philosophy, desire, and curiosity needed to do the job. I've given you the knowledge you need to be successful in this life. The blanks'll be filled when it's time."

"Yeah, but . . . I don't know what to say. I'm sure I've got a million questions. What do I need to do?"

"Simply continue as you have by learning, growing, and expressing yourself in service to others. When your mission in this life is complete, the teapot will become your vessel."

"I'm speechless, Oscar. I don't know what to say."

"Try saying yes."

"Yeah, but . . . What about Karen and everything in this life?"

"Nothing in this life, including those you love and care about, will be affected by your decision. This life is finite and will end regardless of whether or not you accept my offer."

"So what happens if I do? How does it work?"

"At the time your life has run its course, your body will be transformed into elementary particles that mediate the force of gravitation in the framework of the quantum field."

"Huh?"

"You'll be able to navigate curved space-time."

"Oh. So what happens if I don't? Where will I go? Is there an afterlife?"

"Of course. But, just like you, I won't know anything about it until I cross over."

"So how will I know when I have an assignment, or where to go, or how to get there?"

"The teapot spits you out exactly when and where you need to be. You'll instinctively know who your assignment is and the basic nature of his or her problem."

"I'll be immortal too?"

"It's not exactly immortality. You'll become immune to aging and the diseases that go with it. However, you'll still be flesh and blood. Walk in front of a bus, and you'll be a red stain just like the next guy would," he says sternly. "So what do you say?"

"Curved space-time, eh?" I respond, realizing he's offering me the key to knowledge about the workings of our universe that the brightest minds in science have sought for ages.

He nods his head.

"If I'll be able to help others the way you've helped me, then the answer is yes," I reply, reaching out to shake Oscar's hand.

"You've got that ability right now kid. The only difference is that you choose your assignments in this life. Once it's over, the teapot chooses them for you. Speaking of which, I trust you've been keeping the teapot safe?"

"Yeah."

"Good. Here, you'll be needing this."

Oscar brings an old book out from under the table and hands it to me. It must be thousands of years old, like something out of a museum. I take the book with the same care I would have if he had handed me a newborn baby. I'm immediately drawn to the cover.

"What is this?"

"The operator's manual."

"Oscar, this is beautiful. What's this made of?"

"The pages are papyrus. I think it's bound in lambskin. When Arkad gave it to me, he said that lettering is the highest quality gold leaf," he answers, referring to the title on the cover.

I can't take my eyes off of it. The words are written in some kind of ancient language, but I understand them perfectly. The cover reads *Negotiating Curved Space-Time for the Advanced Soul.*

"So you weren't kidding. There really is a handbook! Oscar, this must be priceless. How am I supposed to take care of this thing?"

"You don't. It pretty much takes care of you. Watch. Put the book down."

"As instructed, I gently place the book on the table. After a few seconds, the book dissolves into something like sand and then completely evaporates."

"My heart nearly stopped the first time I saw it do that," Oscar says calmly.

"Where did it go?"

"Back in the teapot. It's in the den on the bookshelf, to the right of the fireplace."

"How do I get it back?"

"Just place your right palm on the lid of the teapot for about three seconds, and it appears. It also has a funny way of appearing on its own, just when it's needed. Once you move in, though, it'll be in the den."

"How do I get inside the teapot?"

"Until it's your time, you can't. But in about fifty or sixty years, you'll find yourself inside. I'll leave some smokes in the humidor for you." He stops to look at his watch. "Well, kid, it's been a pleasure."

"So where do you go from here, Oscar?" I ask, trying to hide the fact that I'm distraught at the thought of losing my friend again.

"First, I'm gonna take a tour of the twenty-first century. An awful lot's changed since my last assignment sixty or so years ago. I'll have to get me one of those doo-dads you got and do some of that googling stuff. Once that's out of my system, I'll return to my vessel. In the meantime, I expect you to mind it while I'm gone."

"I will. Its tucked away safe in our linen closet." I bite my lower lip to keep it from quivering. "Hey, Oscar, I know we haven't known each other for very long, but, well, you're about the best friend I've ever had. Am I ever going to see you again?"

"Oh jeez, there ya go gettin' all sentimental. Look, you're not a bad mug yourself. Tell you what, how's about we get together for another cigar when I get back?"

"I'd like that."

TWENTY-ONE

Severe Obstructive What?

"Tyler? Tyler? Can you hear me?"

Where am I? I can't speak. I can't swallow. There's something in my throat.

"Tyler, I'm Doctor Zadini. You're in the intensive care unit at OHSU hospital. You had a close call, but you're going to be all right. I know these tubes are uncomfortable. We'll have them out in just a few minutes."

How the hell did I get here? I was just in the Tea Zone with Oscar. What's going on?

"Please don't try to speak. Just relax. Tyler, you were found unconscious. The paramedics got to you in time. You had an episode of very low blood oxygen."

What's this guy talking about? How do you have an episode of low blood oxygen?

"Your wife is here. She wants to see you."

"Tyler? Oh baby, I'm sorry. It's my fault this happened."

Okay, what the hell is she talking about?

"Now, now, Mrs. Cirella, this was no one's fault. We've caught it, and we can treat it."

Treat what? I gotta get out of here. Get this thing out of my throat!

"Please, Tyler. Just stay still. I know the tubes are uncomfortable," the doctor says.

"Tyler, it's Karen. Baby, they found you unconscious in the Tea Zone. You weren't breathing."

Right, the Tea Zone. I was just there a second ago with Oscar and . . . Oh jeez, who's this baboon? A guy in scrubs who looks like a competitor in the Steroid Olympics is hovering over me.

"Tyler, this is Uri. He's a nurse. He's going to remove your breathing tube. Your throat might be a bit sore when it's out. This is going to be a little uncomfortable, but it'll be over quickly."

I have to fight to keep from puking as I gag and cough.

"Tyler, are you okay?" Karen asks.

"Yeah," I wheeze. "That's only the second most uncomfortable violation of my body I've ever experienced."

Karen turns to the doctor and rolls her eyes. "He's okay."

"What happened to me?"

"Tyler, I suspect you have a condition known as severe obstructive sleep apnea," the doctor answers.

"Severe obstructive what?"

"Sleep apnea. It can be very serious, in fact fatal. Fortunately you were in a public place when you fell asleep. In serious cases, it can stop your breathing long enough to prevent you from waking. Unless someone is there to wake you up in time, it can be fatal. Fortunately you were discovered in time."

"Sweetie," Karen says, wiping tears from her eyes, "You've had this problem for some time. Every night you snore like a thunderstorm, and then you just stop. I didn't realize you actually stopped breathing."

"Tyler, Karen tells me you suffer from migraines. That's a common symptom in sleep apnea sufferers. It's caused by hypoxia of the brain. Extreme fatigue and hallucinations are not uncommon either. I understand you've been experiencing all of those symptoms."

"Yeah, I guess I have."

"We're going to keep you overnight for observation. That'll also give us a chance to run a sleep study. We're going to try a continuous positive airway pressure device on you tonight, and see if that allows you to breathe. It's called a CPAP for short. However, I've only seen a couple of cases as severe as yours. In both cases, corrective surgery was required. An ENT specialist has been called in to evaluate you. I'm pretty certain he's going to recommend upper respiratory tract reconstruction."

"That sounds unpleasant."

"Perhaps, but if he does recommend it, you'll be a new man once it's over."

TWENTY-TWO

Sunday Morning High Tea

It's a wet and gloomy late Sunday morning. Karen and I are sitting in the lounge at the Tea Zone for high tea.

Karen insisted we get rid of the teapot. But I'm having a very hard time letting go of the idea that Oscar is real and that he does live in there. So I talked her into bringing it back to the Tea Zone. Even though it's dented, I think it still makes a nice display piece. Karen says it belongs in the garbage.

Coming here today also gives me the chance to apologize for the disruption I caused the day they found me unconscious here in the lounge, and to thank Grant and Janie for getting me help in time. My throat's still raw from the first of the three surgeries I have to go through to correct my sleep apnea. At least I can swallow now, long as it's not anything too hot.

"So where is everybody?" Karen asks. "We had to make reservations because high tea here is so popular? There's no one here."

"Yeah, that is strange," I respond. You know, usually this place is packed. In fact . . ."

"What?"

"Well, the only times I've been here when it was empty like this is when Oscar showed up."

"Okay, now that's enough of that. Tyler, it was a figment of your imagination. We know what caused it, and it's being corrected. You can't stay emotionally attached to a hallucination."

Yeah I can, I think to myself. But it's not worth arguing over.

"So, is this thing going to sit here while we eat?" Karen asks, referring to the teapot sitting on the table. "I thought you were going to give it back to them."

"I'll ask them if they want it back when we leave."

"Tyler, I've had enough of this." Karen scolds in a loud whisper. "It's just an ugly teapot. If you won't return it, I will. And if they don't want it, it's going in the trash."

In a huff Karen gets up from the table. She picks up the teapot, lets out a scream, and drops it. Amazingly, it lands perfectly upright on the table.

"What's wrong?"

"Tyler, that thing shocked me!"

She grabs my arm and screams again. "Karen, what the heck is wrong with you?"

"When I touched your arm, you shocked me."

"I shocked you?"

"Yes! Tyler, what the hell is going—" She grows strangely silent, and her eyes open wider than I would have thought anatomically possible. With a gasp, she points at the teapot.

A cloud of mist begins to pour out of the spout. She grabs my arm again, but this time holds on. The walls of the lounge seem to be pulling away from us, like we're getting smaller. The cloud grows and boils, changing colors from a kind of purple, to blue, and then dark gray. There's that strange odor, like frankincense. The mist fills the room and becomes so thick we can't see each other or anything else.

"Tyler, get me out of here!"

The mist begins to dissolve away with the same noise as before, like millions of tiny carbonated bubbles fizzing away. And there, next to the teapot, sits the book Oscar gave me.

Karen sits down, stares at the book, and then back at me. "What? What is that?"

"It's called *Negotiating Curved Space-Time for the Advanced Soul*," I reply nonchalantly. "Oscar told me it would appear when I needed it."

I pick up the book and set it on the table in front of us. After a moment it dissolves into sand and evaporates. I pick up the teapot and say to Karen, "I've decided I'd like to hold on to this. I assume you no longer have a problem with it coming back home with us?"

She just sits with her mouth open without answering.

I place it on the seat next to me, and then pick up the carafe sitting on the table between us and ask, "Care for more tea?"

Appendix

Be sure to check out the businesses named in the story. They're great places to hang out and network!

The Tea Zone
510 NW 11th Ave,
Portland, OR 97209
www.teazone.com

Broadway Cigar Co. (Lake Oswego Lounge)
15561 Boones Ferry Rd
Lake Oswego, OR 97035
www.broadwaycigar.com

Oregon Culinary Institute Restaurant
1701 SW Jefferson St., Portland OR 9720
www.oregonculinaryinstitute.com/restaurant

Portland Business Alliance
200 S.W. Market Street, Suite 150
Portland, OR 97201
www.portlandalliance.com

Powell's City of Books
1005 W Burnside St.
Portland, OR 97209
www.powells.com

World Cup Coffee
Located Inside Powell's Books
www.worldcupcoffee.com/cafes/powells

About the Author

A welder and metal-fitter by trade, Mark Herdering found himself in a mid-life career transition after the collapse of the Southern California aerospace industry and struggled for years to make a living in traditional sales.

Given the option of being fired or hitting a sales goal of $150,000 within 30 days, Mark tried a unique approach which not only resulted in reaching that sales goal but becoming one of the top producers in the office.

Two years later Mark left that job and started an an independent distributorship with a small start-up company that was housed in a garage, marketing 62 cent per-unit greeting cards. In less than three years his business was generating over $1,000,000 in annual revenue . . . all by referral.

In September of 2007 Mark relocated to Portland, Oregon where he continues to build his business. He also serves on the Presidents Council of the Portland Business Alliance.

In 2011 Mark founded PDX Group, a mastermind community of business experts, consultants and business-to-business service providers passionately dedicated to serving the business community through strategic referrals and introductions.

Today Mark speaks across the country, educating business owners and those responsible for outside business development about how to generate referral-based business.

www.hangingoutforaliving.com

9231340R00122